HALBE
1945

HALBE
1945
EYEWITNESS ACCOUNTS FROM
HELL'S CAULDRON

EBERHARD BAUMGART
INTRODUCED BY ROGER MOORHOUSE

TRANSLATED BY EVA BURKE

Greenhill Books

Halbe 1945
First English-language edition
published in 2022 by
Greenhill Books,
c/o Pen & Sword Books Ltd,
47 Church Street, Barnsley,
S. Yorkshire, S70 2AS

www.greenhillbooks.com
contact@greenhillbooks.com

ISBN: 978–1–78438–711–2

Originally published in German as
Halbe 1945: Durchbruch in den Untergang
© 1999 Druffel-Verlag,
Berg am Stranberger See

This edition © Greenhill Books, 2022
Roger Moorhouse introduction © Greenhill Books, 2022

CIP data records for this title are available from the British Library

Designed and typeset by Donald Sommerville

Typeset in 12.2/16.5 pt Minion Pro

Printed and bound in Great Britain by
CPI Group (UK) Ltd, Croydon, CR0 4YY

Contents

Introduction

Halbe 1945: Break-out to Defeat

The Battle of Halbe is not one that holds much resonance for non-German audiences. As the last major engagement of World War Two in Europe, it is conventionally merged with the wider Battle for Berlin, or folded into the general German collapse in the final weeks of the war. Yet, it has a significant story to tell, a bloody, brutal story.

Halbe was the last great encirclement battle of the European war. The encirclement battle was a tactic that resulted when highly mobile forces found an overwhelming advantage in numbers or mobility *vis à vis* their opponents, and consequently it had featured right from the outset of the war, the first being the Battle of Tuchola Heath, in the opening days of September 1939. Such engagements had then seen their hideous apogee in the weeks after the German invasion of the Soviet Union in the summer of 1941, when entire Soviet armies were destroyed in huge encirclements, such as at Minsk, Bryansk and Kiev, and had duly featured once the tide had turned on the Eastern Front, with Red Army forces now encircling the Germans, the most infamous example, perhaps, being Operation Uranus, during the Battle of Stalingrad in November 1942. By 1945, then, encirclement tactics were routinely being deployed against understrength German units, and at Halbe it was against those units that were desperately trying to defend the approaches to Berlin. Halbe, therefore, was grimly symbolic of the war's changes of fortune.

Halbe itself is a small town, not far from the picturesque lakeland of the Spree Forest, south-east of Berlin, but in the spring of 1945 it stood at the heart of an area occupied by the German Ninth Army, under the command of General Theodor Busse. Having already been mauled in the Battle of Seelow Heights, to the east of Berlin, earlier that month, Busse's men now found themselves in the eye of a new Soviet storm; caught between the jaws of two approaching Red Army fronts – with Marshal Georgi Zhukov's 1st Belorussian Front approaching from the north-east, and Marshal Ivan Koniev's 1st Ukrainian Front circling to their rear, heading north-west towards the German capital. Their orders were to attempt to break out, westward, to join up with the German Twelfth Army, under General Walther Wenck, which was fighting the Americans to the south-west of Berlin.

It was a task that was easier said than done. Busse's forces had already been eviscerated, and though they contained a number of SS detachments – including the IX SS Panzer Corps – there were also some much less fearsome units present, some comprising of dragooned Luftwaffe ground crews, and the old men and boys of the Volkssturm – which, though touted as a fearsome *levée en masse*, was in reality little more than a Hitlerite 'Dad's Army'. Busse could field only around 80,000 men, to face a battle-hardened Red Army force more than three times that size.

The clash that ensued matched any of the European war for brutality. As Busse's forces inched westward, using those armoured SS spearheads as a vanguard, they had to maintain a fighting retreat at their rear, to fend off Zhukov's men in the east. Three break-outs were attempted, all of which were contained by the Soviets, with heavy losses on both sides. For those in the centre of the 'cauldron', life was little easier as they endured constant air and artillery attack. As one regimental commander later recalled, the shelling was so intense that he could barely raise his head: 'All I could do was lie under a tank with my adjutant and look at the map.'* In this way, German forces would be contained and systematically reduced.

Barely 20,000 men escaped the Halbe cauldron, making their way in dribs and drabs through the Soviet lines to join up with Wenck's Twelfth Army, which would, in time, surrender to the Americans. The remainder were either captured by the Soviets, or killed. Among the former, there were some significant names, including Obergruppenführer Matthias Kleinheisterkamp, commander of the IX SS Panzer Corps, and the thoroughly odious Obergruppenführer Friedrich Jeckeln, who as commander of one of the infamous *Einsatzgruppen* had been responsible for the cold-blooded murder of over 100,000 Jews earlier in the war. Kleinheisterkamp is thought to have committed suicide, Jeckeln would be hanged for his crimes. One who survived the carnage was Colonel Hans von Luck, whose capture brought to an end a remarkable military career, which had spanned Poland in 1939, France in 1940, Operation Barbarossa, North Africa and Normandy.† Some 30,000 German soldiers did not survive Halbe – a figure broadly comparable in scale to the entire Allied death toll in the Battle for Normandy of 1944. In addition, an estimated 20,000 Soviet soldiers were killed, as well as around 10,000 civilian dead. Halbe, clearly, was no side-show.

*

---

* Quoted in Antony Beevor, *Berlin: The Downfall 1945* (London, 2002), p. 332.
† See Hans von Luck, *Panzer Commander* (London, 1989).

This collection of first-hand accounts tells the story of the battle and its aftermath, from the German perspective. It is an eclectic mix, containing the recollections of ordinary soldiers, from enlisted men to senior officers, and civilians, as well as SS men, men of the Panzer divisions, even the former mayor of Halbe himself. It brings to life the grim realities of this most one-sided engagement and contains numerous harrowing vignettes highlighting the ever-present threat of the brutal vengeance of the Soviets, the Red Army's material superiority, and the desperation just to escape the slaughter.

Interestingly, some of the accounts presented here make reference to so-called 'Seydlitz Troops' – German POWs who had been 'turned' by the Soviets and were now sent behind German lines to sow disinformation and chaos. In truth, 'Seydlitz Troops', which were named after a German POW of the Soviets, General Walther von Seydlitz-Kurbach, were a figment of the fevered German imagination of 1945. Though Seydlitz was a prominent mouthpiece for Red Army propaganda aimed at German soldiers, such troops were never given the operational go-ahead by Stalin, and there is no evidence beyond the anecdotal that they ever fought. It is, perhaps, testament to the desperation that many German soldiers and civilians felt, in the maelstrom of war that resulted in Halbe, that so many of them appear to have believed in such a chimera.

Aside from the vicarious, visceral thrill of reading such accounts, one must bear in mind that they have a purpose. The Battle of Halbe scarcely registers with most readers, even those rather well-versed in the intricacies of World War Two in Europe. In addition, most of those who write the histories that we read regrettably lack the language skills necessary to access new material and original sources. Consequently, events like the Battle of Halbe struggle to penetrate the established narrative, and so continue to languish in comparative obscurity, until a volume such as this one presents an opportunity for change; for a shift, however modest, in the story. This is to be welcomed. However difficult the subject matter, however discomfiting the stories portrayed, it is only through bringing such material to a wider public that progress is made towards a more comprehensive understanding of history.

For all that, however, what comes across most strongly is the sense of human tragedy in evidence on these pages; the rapes, the murdered prisoners, the wanton cruelty. The spectacle of the forces of two hideous totalitarian regimes fighting to the death, with no quarter given or expected – just as no quarter had been given or expected when the Germans had been supremely dominant some three years earlier – is one that should give us all pause, and should encourage us to cherish the fact that we live in more peaceful times.

Roger Moorhouse

Translator's Note

The bulk of this book consists of memories or diary notes written by eye-witnesses of the battles in and around Halbe in 1945, during the campaign that saw the downfall of Berlin. As such, these first-hand accounts are written in different registers as the authors vary in age and background. Some are military personnel, from high-ranking SS men to ordinary *Landser*. Some are bystanders, ordinary civilian men and women; others are landowners and farmers. Often, we hear the voice of the town mayor. The text – though replete with army talk that lays bare a lack of leadership and absence of strategic thinking – is overlaid with a vocabulary primarily conveying pain, disappointment and defeat.

Out of touch or vaguely worded orders handed down by the Nazi leadership reflect the total collapse of their war which is echoed by troops being confused, indecisive and ignorant as to what to do, when and where. The lack of maps on the German side is felt in unclear, often conflicting directions given and received. The tone and language used by the Nazi regime to have their people and armed forces believe in victory – yet in the end causing death and destruction in their own midst – reminds one instinctively of that used by the Nazi regime in its propaganda and extermination drives against minorities: purposely devious, intentionally misleading, deliberately hiding behind language intended to keep victims in the dark, and perpetrators firmly believing in a distorted reality. There was a collapse of language which, with heavy irony, then played itself out to the detriment of the Nazi regime's own people.

I decided not to focus on consistency of tenses nor did I elaborate on geographical references made by the authors, so as to offer to the reader an authentic sense of time suspended and a blurred recollection of space.

Repetitions – various chroniclers recall the same event more than once – have not been edited out. The intention here is to suggest that while recollections of time and space were hazy, the sense of trauma was prevalent and true.

The last part of the book consists of some of the compiler's own thoughts in the aftermath of the Battle of Halbe, specifically with reference to how and when those killed were buried and what happened to the survivors. What was the role the Soviet leadership played with respect to the war cemeteries and the camps they erected for their prisoners of war? These were often referred to as *Schweigelager* (silence camps) because the inmates were not permitted to have contact with the outside world. Here, it wasn't the disintegration or collapse of language that governed communication but rather its total absence. This 'silence' deliberately concealed the Soviet power's inhumane, cruel, torturous and murderous treatment of prisoners and the atrocious conditions they were kept in. The compiler makes reference to that. This silence also obliterated any information about the prisoners. What had been their military career? What had been their involvement on the Eastern Front? Here too, the compiler often fills in the vacuum, albeit rather too selectively, leaving the dark side of the Wehrmacht's activities blank and instead highlighting his intense dislike of Communist ideologies.

I omitted the *ex-* which the compiler and author inserted before a contributor's wartime Wehrmacht or SS title, as these men were never removed from their position, nor absolved of their actions. Thus, they appear as Hauptsturmführer and not ex-Hauptsturmführer.

Eva Burke

THE EYEWITNESS ACCOUNTS

Dear visitor,

When you come to Halbe, consider this:

You are at the site of the largest burial ground in all of modern Germany's history!

Remember the fallen. Consider that they were not only soldiers, but women and children too, who died during their so-called 'liberation' by the Soviets!

Lakes and dense forests dominate the landscape of Mark Brandenburg
south-east of Berlin, creating bottlenecks on the
German retreat routes in 1945.

'Geography is a Law which Governs History'
Attributed to Cervantes

This quote came true with the tragic and bloody destruction of the Ninth Army, an army which retreated to the south-west over the Berlin–Frankfurt/Oder highway with its left flank completely destroyed but whose general, Theodor Busse, showed himself utterly inflexible when it came to strategy. Intent on refusing either to be pushed or ordered back into an encircled Berlin under any circumstances, he also had no wish to capitulate and offer up his army to the Soviets. His only other option then was to pass round Berlin to the south-west and, by reaching the safety of the Elbe river, link up with Walther Wenck's Twelfth Army.

Slipping through tight gaps in a neck of land bounded by a chain of lakes south of the highway, the units that were forced back would find themselves in a large heavily forested region, a cauldron with its southern edge bordering on the impenetrable Spreewald and traversed by the Dahme river. The only break-out route led through a bottleneck-shaped piece of countryside with no lakes.

The Route through Halbe

Those managing to traverse this corridor ended up in a dense forest, enclosed on all sides, with its southern border made up by the Baruth glacial valley which points west and only west. Two *Reichsautobahnen*, four *Reichsstrassen* and the same number of rail lines cut through this crescent-shaped woodland from north to south offering those surrounding the pocket ideal lines of advance. The Soviet chief of staff had done his homework and, having studied the geography of this area in depth, was in full control and able to exercise command on both a strategic and tactical level. Soviet resources extended, of course, to the German communist scouts operating undercover who were well equipped to put themselves to 'good use'.

It so happened that when it came to cartography the encircled German troops were groping in the dark, often quite literally. Not a single officer in the lower ranks of the army reported

The course of the Dahme not far from Märkisch Buchholz, another obstacle in the face of the Ninth Army's retreat.

having had any maps to hand. Even the commander of the '30th January' SS Division, charged with providing cover to the Ninth Army retreating from the Halbe cauldron, was completely out of his depth and unaware of what was going on. Only one small unit reports that it had been fortunate enough to acquire a ramblers' map of the area which outlined an escape route along a trail penetrating the forest and then to the safety of the opposite bank of the Elbe.

The Halbe bottleneck became a fateful pit swallowing up tens of thousands of men . . .

Opposing Forces in the Battle of Halbe

Red Army
45 rifle divisions, 13 tank/armoured brigades 1 artillery division

Wehrmacht
11 infantry divisions, 2 motorised divisions, 1 tank division

At the beginning of the Battle of Berlin (16 April 1945) German divisions were reduced to an average combat force of 5,000 soldiers and the above matchup shows the vast, indeed four-fold, Russian superiority in available units: a ratio of 45 to 11 infantry divisions. Additionally, the German forces would lose much of their heavy armour in the course of their retreat and were running dangerously low on fuel and lubricants. The troops' morale had dropped precipitously and wounded and sick German bodies heaped on the ground could barely be attended to (a 50 per cent casualty rate was registered). Also, fuelled by Nazi propaganda, the Germans were terrified of what would happen if Berlin fell into Soviet hands.

Contrasting the dismal picture on the German side, the Soviet situation was impressive. With Soviet troops highly motivated, tightly organized and well equipped with heavy weapons of all sizes, their thrusts were keenly coordinated; in addition, they had a highly efficient system in place for recovering their wounded. If this were not enough, the 1st Ukrainian Front was well informed about the local geography and its men were able to construct elaborate ambush positions along the German line of retreat that would enable them to inflict heavy casualties. Wenck's Twelfth Army was thinly strung out to the west with sometimes only a handful of soldiers holding a kilometre of the front line.

Red Army Psychological Warfare

Willi Haenecke, ex-mayor of Halbe

The following steps were taken to encourage troops of the Ninth Army to capitulate:

- 1st Ukrainian Front dropped some 4 million propaganda flyers.
- Hundreds of loudspeakers positioned just behind the front line blared out invitations to surrender.
- Turncoat prisoners of war working for the Red Army against their former comrades were often sent back (to the German side) to incite and agitate.
- Specially trained civilians from the battle zone, men and women, were sent to infiltrate German positions. (A total of 861 prisoners were sent to the

A typical forest track. The Mark Brandenburg woods seemed to offer safety and shelter for the fugitives but for many it became their last resting place.

———

German side. Some 477 of these went back to the Russians – taking with them 8,816 defectors.)

- So-called Seydlitz units (supposedly operating on behalf of the National Committee for a Free Germany[*]) were present, camouflaged in Wehrmacht uniforms.

———

[*] The Nationalkomitee Freies Deutschland, or NKFD, was a Soviet-controlled anti-Nazi organisation of German exiles.

After some initial break-outs the situation of the Ninth Army turned catastrophic. Effectively deprived of any leeway to act, it possessed only the barest minimum of ammunition for its heavy weapons and had severe shortages of fuel for its tanks and trucks. Troops were reduced to close-quarter fighting with little more than small arms. A thinly spread line of tanks and assault guns with a pathetic number of shells provided the backbone of the German operations and were thus far more exposed to the ferocious enemy fire. Nearly all of them were destroyed.

The Soviet troops – so close to victory – were highly motivated. The other side of the coin was, however, the fact that not a single one of them wished to die a hero's death. Later German eyewitness accounts comment on how carefully Soviet infantry behaved on the raging battlefield as they knew full well that whichever way this attack ended, 'Fritz' wasn't going to slip through their fingers.

Deafening Noises reach Halbe

Willi Haenecke, ex-mayor of Halbe

In the summer of 1944, the Allies embarked on their invasion of the Atlantic coast. While the war was already lost, many people refused to believe this to be true or put on a show of confidence to calm each other down.

In Halbe, as in the Reich as a whole, a provisional militia, the Volkssturm, was formed from October 1944 with all men

An Allied propaganda newspaper reports the Anglo-American crossing of the Rhine and Soviet successes in the East. The Rhine crossing caused Stalin to speed up his assault on Berlin

Neue Waffe SEITE 4

Frontpost

„Der Starke braucht die Wahrheit nicht zu scheuen."
Ernst Moritz Arndt

März Nr. 3

Nummer 51 — 12. HG

NACHRICHTEN FÜR DEUTSCHE SOLDATEN. HERAUSGEBER: DIE AMERIKANISCHEN TRUPPEN IN WESTEUROPA

Amerikaner über den Rhein

PARIS. — Amerikanische Truppen haben bei Remagen den Rhein überschritten und auf dem Ostufer einen Brückenkopf gebildet. Das linksrheinische Ufer von Nijmegen bis vor Koblenz, in einer Länge von 320 km, ist in alliierter Hand. Im Raum Andernach wurden 6 deutsche Divisionen eingekesselt.

Bonn erobert — Wesel-Brückenkopf vernichtet

Die amerikanische Erste Armee, die Köln erobert hatte, erreichte in raschem Vorstoß Remagen, überraschte die deutsche Besatzung, die die Rheinbrücke sprengen sollte, und stürmte über den Rhein. Innerhalb weniger Tage wurde der amerikanische Brückenkopf am rechtsrheinischen Ufer zu einer festen Stellung von 15 km Breite und 5 km Tiefe ausgebaut, die das Ufer beherrschenden Höhen wurden erobert, und die Städte Linz, Rheinbreitbach, Bruchhausen und Ohlenburg genommen. In Honnef wird gekämpft.

Xanten genommen

Am Nordabschnitt der Westfront vernichteten die kanadische Erste und die britische Zweite Armee der deutschen Brückenkopf bei Wesel, der von deutschen Fallschirmjägern verzweifelt verteidigt worden war. Der deutsche Stützpunkt Xanten wurde erobert. Das westliche Ufer des Rheins ist von Nijmegen bis kurz vor Koblenz in alliierter Hand.

Kessel bei Andernach

Truppen der amerikanischen Ersten und Dritten Armee haben sich bei Andernach vereinigt, die Stadt genommen, und 6 deutsche Divisionen, die sich noch auf der linken Seite des Rheines befanden, eingekesselt. Tausende

de deutscher Soldaten und Offiziere haben hier und an anderen Stellen der Westfront den Kampf eingestellt. Seit Beginn der alliierten Rheinlandoffensive am 23. Februar haben 108 620 Deutsche den Widerstand aufgegeben.

Das industrielle Herz Deutschlands, das Ruhrgebiet, liegt unter schwerem Luft- und Artilleriebombardement.

Essen, Duisburg und Düsseldorf werden vom linksrheinischen Ufer beschossen. Britische und amerikanische schwere Bomber haben militärische und industrielle Ziele in Essen, Bremen, Hamburg, Kassel, Münster, Osnabrück, Frankfurt am Main und Dessau angegriffen. Berlin wird seit über drei Wochen allnächtlich von RAF-Schnellbombern bombardiert.

Acht alliierte Armeen

Eine neue amerikanische Armee, die Fünfzehnte, ist an der Westfront eingesetzt worden. Die Alliierten haben jetzt acht Armeen an der Westfront im Einsatz.

Auf der deutschen Seite dagegen haben die Erste Fallschirmjäger-Armee und die deutsche Fünfzehnte Armee so schwere Verluste erlitten, daß sie als Kampfeinheiten zu bestehen aufgehört haben. Die Alliierten haben in der Schlacht ums Rheinland einen vollen Sieg errungen.

Russen erobern Küstrin

MOSKAU. — Marschall Stalin hat in einem Tagesbefehl bekannt gegeben, daß Truppen der Heeresgruppe Zhukov die Festung Küstrin an der Oder erobert haben. Küstrin war der wichtigste Punkt im Verteidigungssystem der Deutschen im östlichen Vorfeld von Berlin und beherrschte den Übergang über die Oder.

Sowjets an der Odermündung bei Stettin

Der rechte Flügel der Heeresgruppe Zhukov hat die Außenbezirke von Stettin erreicht und Deutschlands wichtigster Ostseehafen ist unter Artilleriebeschuß. Die Russen sind in der Vorstadt Altdam, an der Mündung der Oder ins Stettiner Haff eingedrungen. Cammin, Gollnow und Stepenitz wurden erobert.

Russen in den Vororten von Danzig

Truppen der Heeresgruppe Rokossovsky haben Danzig vom Rest des Reiches abgeschnitten und stehen zwischen Danzig und Gdingen knapp vor der Danziger Bucht. Sie sind in den Vororten von Danzig eingedrungen, und die Stadt liegt unter Artilleriebeschuß. Meisterwalde wurde erobert. Zwischen Danzig und Stettin haben die Russen fast ganz Pommern bis zur Ostsee genommen. Die befestigten Stützpunkte Leba, Lauenburg, Stolpmünde, Stolp, Schlawe und Rügenwalde wurden genommen. In Kolberg wird gekämpft. In Ungarn greifen die Deutschen im Raum des Plattensees an in dem Bestreben, zur Donau durchzubrechen. Die Angriffe der Deutschen wurden blutig abgewiesen. An einem einzigen Tag wurden 162 deutsche Panzer abgeschossen.

between the ages of sixteen and sixty called up to register at the local town hall. I was one of those waiting in line.

The Red Army reached the banks of the Oder early in 1945. The Volkssturm was sworn in. We were trained in how to operate a Panzerfaust and once I even got the chance to fire one. This, I asked myself incredulously holding the launch tube in my hand, is supposed to do the trick and hold off the Soviets? One of our units was charged to construct defensive positions in Halbe: we dug foxholes and laid anti-tank defences all around the city.

Halbe itself had to face its own challenge: housing a stream of refugees with some 1,000 passing through every night. Many of them arrived with carts brimming over with whatever possessions these people had managed to gather before fleeing their homes; others just pulled along a sparsely filled hand-wagon. Each morning they were ordered to move on and make way for the next batch. Few of them had a destination in mind. 'West' was the single word etched in their consciousness.

Understandably, ever since January 1945 the population had been feeling increasingly worried. With the daily din of shelling and explosions near the Oder growing to a crescendo, the question on everyone's lips was: 'What'll happen to us? Where should we flee to?'

Then one day, our two French workers said to me in broken German: 'Boss, you getting two large crates. You putting in all valuables – you then bury it.' They were, truth be told, better informed than we had realised. It is thanks to them that we managed to salvage enough to keep us going for a while after the war. Some horse dealers, including myself, had considered setting off westwards.

Otto Buchwald, a bar owner and also a trader in horses like me, planned to go along with the retreating troops by using the forest path leading to Baruth. At the time, none of us knew that the Red Army had occupied Baruth, Wünsdorf and Zossen and that in actual fact we were surrounded. I had covered two carts with a tarpaulin and was intending to harness a horse to one of them for my parents. For one reason or another we kept delaying our departure and, fortunately for us, this turned out to be the right decision.

It transpired that our friends the Paulitz family would pay dearly for their flight. While they managed to travel without any hassle from the Buchwalds' place to the Autobahn, they then realised too late that it had already fallen into the hands of the Red Army. (The loss of civilian life this entailed was horrendous.) Frau Buchwald was able to escape to Baruth and then return several weeks later, but Herr Buchwald and the Paulitz family fled to Halbe with Frau Paulitz being shot dead en route. Herr Buchwald, heavily wounded, sought refuge in his cellar, but his wagon and his animals were gone.

Like my predecessor Schiebe I tried to ensure that the Volkssturm stored their weapons in a stable on the lower level of the town hall. In truth, I had no authority to give any such commands, but by then everyone had realised that it was sheer folly to put up any resistance.

I kept turning over and over in my mind what I was meant to do. Should I attempt to break away, at some point, somehow? Surely, I would be able to return once all had calmed down. Before too long I had packed my rucksack, stuffed it with food and set off. As I passed Löptner Strasse near Mastrangelos a woman stopped to ask me where I was headed. When I admitted that indeed I had no idea, she offered to help. 'Why don't you stay the night . . . perhaps it won't be as bad as you fear.' I decided to do just that, never dreaming that this particular night would determine my fate. I decided to stay put and not flee . . .

Seydlitz Troops

Hauptsturmführer Hohengassner, SS Anti-Aircraft Division 550

On 25 April 1945 our squad was redistributed to the area of Hermsdorf–Forstamt Hammer. It was at the time when the enemy put the lid on the Halbe cauldron – we were completely encircled ... The enemy hammered us with an irresistible ferocity, deploying supporters of the National Committee for a Free Germany who were charged to cause confusion amongst German troops.

This is when we first came across Seydlitz troops and realised what their intentions were. Men in fake officers' uniforms began to appear more and more frequently, mingling amongst our troops and issuing what struck us as the most impossible orders, which they presented to us as commands from higher up. These fabricated instructions had a devastating impact. They varied in content and complemented each other: units were not permitted to retreat; they were to gather and convene at assembly points; it was their duty to blow up guns, tanks and other vehicles. Non-compliance with the orders would result in unit leaders being shot immediately, on the spot. One thing these turncoats had in common was that none seemed to cover their heads; they all wore a white armband and sported new uniforms on which were pinned numerous decorations.

Chaos erupted close to the Dahme river. Units thrust forwards from all directions towards its only bridge. Some intended to escape to Wendisch-Buchhold, others to Halbe. Amid the turmoil members of the National Committee for a Free Germany issued conflicting orders as described above ... What followed was total mayhem. Officers took their own lives and men became

SSD-Fernschreiben.　　　　　　　　　13.4.45.　　　68

An
Gen.Kdo. VIII. Fl.Korps　　　　　　Hermannstädtel)
Lg.Kdo. VIII　　　　　　　　　　　Prag-Rusin　)　ohne A.J.
Kdr.d.Lfl.Truppen　　　　　　　　　Senator 11　　)
Lfl.Kdo.6 / II (zugl.für alle dort.　　　　　　　　　　　315
　　　　　　Abteilungen)　　　　Senator 11

　　Folgender Tagesbefehl ist am 2o.4. in würdiger Form
der Truppe bekanntzugeben:

　　　　　　Kameraden der Luftflotte 6!

　　Unser Führer und Oberster Befehlshaber begeht am 2o. April
seinen 56. Geburtstag.

　　Vom Feind bedroht, ringt das deutsche Volk mit aller Kraft
um die Erhaltung seiner Art und Rasse.

　　Deutsches Blut tränkt deutsche Erde; reinen Herzens vergos-
sen; für Deutschlands Größe gläubig dargebracht.

　　Unerschütterlich im Vertrauen auf den Mut, die Weisheit und
den Siegeswillen unseres Führers, umklammern wir die Waffen fester,
packen unsere Hände härter zu. Mehr denn je!

　　Standhaft und treu!

　　Es lebe der Führer!

　　　　　　　　　　　von　G r e i m
　　　　　　　　Generaloberst u. O.B. der Lfl. 6

　　　　　　　　　　　　F.d.R.

Schriftlich an:
Ia
Ic
O.Qu.
Höh.Nafü (zugl.für Ln.-Truppe)
Kdt.d.St.Qu.
KTB
O.B. (E)

A note regarding commemorating Hitler's birthday, from General
von Greim of Luftflotte 6, shortly to be promoted to command the
Luftwaffe as a whole in place of the discredited Hermann Göring.

15

hysterical, running through the open space like hounded prey. Wounded bodies piled up high on the roadside. Indiscriminate Russian fire caused heavy casualties on our side and there was no resistance to speak of. Each one of us was his own commander.

---

28 April 1945: 2200 hours

Excerpt from the diary of Oberscharführer Horst Woycinick, artillery observer with 32nd SS Division '30th January'

In the early hours of 28 April, we were redeployed. To join our division in the pocket of Halbe, we first had to trudge along some six kilometres of marshy terrain, until we finally reached our 4th Battalion. We found ourselves in the proximity of the Hammer forester's lodge where I met up with Obersturmführer Rencher and Sturmbannführer Ernst.

We pulled over beside the narrow forest path. We passed out ammunition to the 4th Battalion and rendered our guns inoperable. After burying the breech blocks and optical equipment from the guns, we then destroyed our vehicles. We hacked apart their radiators and sliced their tyres. The oil spilled into the sand. We also buried all our personal belongings, apart from some food and ammunition.

Good luck had it that on that day rain came pouring down! That meant poor conditions for the Red ground-attack aircraft. We were packed so closely together in the lodge that we were practically suffocating each other. A hit from an enemy bomb would mean certain death. Our gunners and the rocket-launchers of our 4th Battalion pounded the Russian positions. One would have thought that the enemy would buckle under such assaults.

Red Army sub-machine gunners follow in the wake of an attacking T-34/85 tank during the Soviet advance to the Oder at the end of March 1945.

We grabbed enough rations to last us four days and at 2200 it all began. Pent-up feelings of aggression among the masses who were locked in the 'pocket' flared up. Those ready for the break-out crossed the bridge over the Dahme river and rapidly, mindlessly advanced towards the woods, direction south. In order not to lose each other, each one was yelling at the top of his voice; nobody made sense or could think straight. Trained reflexes took over. We could hear the roar of ferocious fighting at the front. Phosphorus shells burst with glowing white splashes illuminated the dark sky – this lasted two hours until midnight.

Marshal Georgi Zhukov, commander of the 1st Belorussian Front in the final battles for Berlin in 1945.

Attack Spurred by Agony

Hauptscharführer Ernst Streng,
502nd Heavy Tank Battalion

This was the last time we experienced such a concentrated fury and such penetrating force, displayed here by the German troops assembled around the Oder. They were prepared for attack and certain death. As I peered down from my turret, I saw soldiers who were smiling. Young enthusiastic lads who were ready to die for their comrades without a second thought, they were intoxicated by our initial success. Thus exhilarated, we men in field grey made good progress.

We rolled past hastily dug positions. Soldiers lay huddled together. Weapons and equipment of all kinds were spread around them . . . Suddenly the silence was pierced by the noise of battle. The lead tank's gun roared and bursts of machine-gun fire hammered into the Russian positions. There's a radio order from Neu: 'Advance guard is to persist, convoys in the rear must be prohibited from accumulating and creating a bottle-neck.' Pressed to the ground by tracer bullets, we could still see the Russians dashing around . . . Tanks smashed past, through the open fields where panicking Russian horses jumped around frantically.

Just short of the edge of the wood on the other side, close to the Löpten farm, we came across a narrow pathway bordered by a light screen of hedges. Approaching, we were greeted by German soldiers climbing out of their foxholes, guns held high above their heads and with an ecstatic and grateful look in their eyes. Rarely have I seen bearded faces lined by such extreme exhaustion peering up at me from underneath their old World War I steel helmets. This German combat unit had gone through unimaginably horrendous circumstances just north of Halbe. Totally cut off from all other friendly troops and fiercely assaulted by surrounding Russian tank and rifle units, they had a negligible chance of getting away let alone achieving victory. The open meadow up to the edge of the wood opposite was completely littered with corpses, none of them yet buried, face downward, hands still clutching in anguish at clumps of earth . . . others on their backs with eyes full of horror turned upwards, arms flung wide . . .

After a short stop we hastened on with other, mostly elderly soldiers who had survived the onslaught joining our convoy. Ahead of us: Halbe!

The Oath of Allegiance Holds No Longer

Heinz Keim, telegraphist, 107th Anti-Aircraft Regiment

Saturday 28 April 1945 – we are released from our pledge. Where? Birkhold near Märkisch Buchholz.

The commander of our 107th Regiment, Oberst Tyroller, along with the operations officer, Lieutenant Frommberger, travelled to a briefing with leaders of other units and the general staff. They had responded to a directive received by intercepted radio

Allies Encircle Stuttgart; Nuremburg Cleared

PARIS EDITION

THE STARS AND STRIPES

Daily Newspaper of U.S. Armed Forces   in the European Theater of Operations

Man Spricht Deutsch		Ici On Parle Français
Waffen niederlegen! Va-fen nee-der-lay-gen! Throw down your arms!		Vous êtes bien aimable. Voos eht boyen climabble. You are very kind.

Vol. 1—No. 268   1 Fr.   1 Fr.—Saturday, April 21, 1945

Reds in Berlin's Suburbs

7th, French Closing On Stuttgart

BULLETIN

NUREMBURG, April 20 (Reuter).—All organized resistance in Nuremburg ended late today.

Gen. Eisenhower's drives against the northern and southern German fronts gained momentum yesterday as his armies on the central sector before Berlin continued to build up for the assault on the capital and the link-up with the Russians.

On the southern front, combined forces of Lt. Gen. Alexander M. Patch's U.S. seventh and Gen. Jean de Lattre de Tassigny's French First Armies were enveloping Stuttgart. One French column struck deep into southern Germany 30 miles from Lake Constance and the Swiss frontier.

In an Order of the Day, Gen. Eisenhower announced that the Battle of the Ruhr had ended with enormous success. Gen. Omar N. Bradley's 12th Army Group eliminated 21 enemy divisions, including three panzer, one parachute and ...

Berlin Worth $1,000 To Some Lucky GI

A prize of $1,000 awaits the first Ottawa County, Okla., GI to reach Berlin, and prove it according to the Veterans of Foreign Wars Post of Miami, Okla.

The organization requests that the Oklahoman submit his name, rank, serial number, and APO number, along with the time of his arrival in the German capital.

A similar award awaits the first Ottawa County GI to reach Tokyo.

Yanks Unleash Vast Drive at Okinawa Japs

GUAM, April 20 (ANS).—The greatest American offensive force ever employed in a single Pacific sector was flung early yesterday against all directly defended Japanese positions along a four-mile front guarding Okinawa's capital city of Naha.

By noon, three U.S. Divisions—the Seventh, 27th and 96th, numbering perhaps 45,000 men—had scored gains of 100 to 200 yards in a campaign which officers conceded would be tough and slow.

Before the big drive started two-day-old artillery, cruisers and other fleet units blasted Martin and Army ...

Nazis Admit Russian Gains; Report U.S.-Soviet Linkup

German sources last night said that Russian troops had entered the defenses of Berlin proper.

Red spearheads were reported to have reached the suburban towns of Hangelsberg and Strausberg, seven and eight miles respectively from the outskirts of the city, German radio said.

Moscow did not elaborate yesterday on its previous announcement that the Oder and Neisse Rivers had been ...

Linkup Reported

Moscow Radio reported last night that Soviet armored columns had contacted U.S. Third Army scouts near Dresden. The report, picked up in New York or International News Service, was not immediately confirmed by either Berlin, Moscow or SHAEF.

... crossed, but unofficial front-line reports reaching Moscow said that two Red armies were pouring over both river barriers and were overhead ...

An edition of the official newspaper of the U.S. armed forces, *Stars and Stripes*, showing the early stages of the development of the Halbe pocket as the advance of 1st Ukrainian Front south-east of Berlin, begins to make ground.

---

message. The destination was an area called Kleinhammer, some 7.5 km north-west of where we were, as the crow flies.

At approximately 1500 hours Oberst Tyroller ordered us to muster in the yard of the command post. Informing us briefly of the hopeless situation, he left us in no doubt that all communication lines with higher headquarters had now been severed. With that, he both declared us relieved of our oath of allegiance and released the Russians we were still holding prisoner. Everyone, so we gathered, was left to his own devices and should muddle through as well as he could to the west, break through either to the Americans or home. He wished us all the best and good luck.

Reduced to a small group of four female Luftwaffe auxiliaries, two of them with their fiancés, and two other soldiers, Gefreiter Klaus Müller and Radioman Günter Siebold, plus myself, we marched west. Some Russians – Hiwis[*] – at the command post felt lost, and not knowing what to do they asked whether they could join us. According to our calculations it was a long way to the Elbe and we had little chance of being able to reach it. We decided that it was best to get rolled up by the Russians at some point, somewhere.

We set off through the pine forest, heading south-west, then continued towards the Köthenersee. That was our first stop and with the help of the Hiwis we dug in. Artillery batteries from the Leibisch area (east of where we were) opened fire on us, making it seem too dangerous for us to remain. Their indiscriminate shelling with ammunition spraying in all directions caused Feldwebel Truschel to be badly injured by a stray bullet and his girl wounded by several splinters in her left arm.

The area around us was packed with SS soldiers. I had already provided first aid, when coincidentally a field ambulance passed by and its crew offered Feldwebel Truschel and Ruth Nowak a ride through the wood to Märkisch Buchholz. There were more injured people sat in the truck. I'm not sure whether my two comrades turned out to be lucky enough to make it to the hospital

---

[*] Hiwis, short for Hilfswilliger, or volunteer helpers, were usually former Soviet soldiers who, after being taken prisoner, had agreed to serve with the German forces, in practice often in combatant units rather than the initially envisaged non-combatant roles.

General der Infanterie Theodor Busse commanded the German Ninth Army during the desperate fighting in the Halbe pocket.

in Märkisch Buchholz. Those of us left behind preferred to push on, putting behind us one or two kilometres by marching south-west and seeking shelter in the thickets beside a path.

It all went to plan. With the help of our Russians we dug out two zigzag trenches, in one of which the Russians hid, and us in the other one. Not counting myself, that made: the Oberwachtmeister (I can't remember his name) with his fiancé Hanne Scholtissek, a Luftwaffe auxiliary called Luci Scherner, my sister-in-law Elfi, Klaus Müller and Günter Siebold. That's where we spent the night. During the night a dud hit the ground close to us, it whizzed through the air, crackled and then, while we waited for it to explode, nothing actually happened. Early the next morning, we saw a crater ripped into the ground some two metres from our trenches.

Towards dawn on 29 April Ivan moved into the forests and, unharmed, we were taken prisoner. The female Luftwaffe auxiliaries were separated from us. I didn't know where they were being taken. What I gathered from the Russian gibberish loudly exchanged between the Hiwis and their compatriots was easily understood from their gesticulations: we would not come to any harm. Unusually, we weren't even ordered to put up our hands, nor did they frisk us. I just ended up handing over to a Russian soldier my P 38, along with three full spare magazines. First he was taken aback, but then he fell into a jig – this had probably never happened to him.

This was the beginning of my time as a Russian prisoner of war. Later on, we actually did catch sight of our Luftwaffe auxiliaries sitting around aimlessly in the Oderin rail station. We had no idea what would happen to them next. We were put up in a field south and south-west of Oderin. We spent the night in the open air, without any food, but most of us still had some rations left in our knapsacks.

Masses of soldiers had gathered there and the members of our small group eventually lost contact with each other. Between 30 April and 2 May 1945, we marched through forests, across boggy country lanes, past the Neuendorfer See and the Scharmützelsee, past Fürstenwald towards Frankfurt/Oder, ending up in what was previously an anti-aircraft barracks. I'd estimate that we were some fifteen or twenty thousand soldiers. All the barracks were full to the brim; many had to sleep out in the open.

Our Assault on Halbe

Marcel Staar, from German-occupied Luxembourg,
had been conscripted by the Wehrmacht

At precisely midnight our battalion departed from Märkisch Buchholz, direction Halbe. A dense layer of cloud obscured the sky, cigarettes had to be extinguished, pipes scraped out. A glimmer would be enough to give us away. No speaking, no clanking with equipment or armament to be heard.

On foot, the distance we had to cover was likely to take about an hour. Cautiously, slowly, we groped our way forwards. We could barely make out the street ahead, what with it being nearly completely dark. After a few hundred metres we veered off to approach our destination from the south via the forest: Halbe train station. Sometimes the moon would shine through a gap in the otherwise thickly clouded sky and the metal parts of our weapons and equipment shimmered in the dim light. A layer of smoke from nearby fires hung above the treetops. High pitched mooing of distressed cattle could be heard through the din of battle. Mortar shells and explosions.

At many points along the edge of the cauldron the earth was flaming red as if ruptured by a volcano. Often, tongues of bright flame rose into the air to then tumble down in luminous flashes. Keep going! In total disarray, but rifles at the ready, we followed a paved path winding its way through the dense forest to the Dahme which wasn't particularly deep or wide. Its water slipped by dark and wistfully, just like all the Mark's tributaries. Crossing via a swaying gangplank, we got to the other side.

The man in front of me, who interpreted every experience as a secret, mystical sign, and was blindly fatalistic, whispered

A Red Army T-34/85 tank passes a column of German prisoners heading into captivity, on the outskirts of Berlin, end of April 1945.

that his death was near: the evil water spirits had revealed it to him. His voice was distorted by horror. I countered that death only catches those who hesitate while good fortune favours the brave. I got encouragement from my own words. Up we went on the slightly sloping path across the Teupitzer Sander, a hill in the Baruth glacial valley. Every step of the way was heavy, laden with exhaustion and weakness. My pulse was racing, my heart pounding. Then, suddenly, approaching from the south-west, we stood just short of Halbe, with the silhouette of its church steeple eerily looming large against the gloomy morning sky. To our right we made out a sawmill with rows of wood planks stacked in front and next to it lay shot-up trucks and burnt tanks. Dawn illuminated the scene in a ghostly fashion. A squadron of bombers roared over our heads . . . We had made it to the assault position.

Ordered to fan out, we then began hastily to dig foxholes. It felt strange, how easily our shovels sank into the soft earth, destroying the first seedlings. We could hear the crunching of pebbles and

A column of truck-borne Soviet infantry passes a heavy assault gun
unit on a forest road in Brandenburg.

before long I crouched down inside, carbine loaded ready to shoot and clamped between my knees, my eyes focused on Halbe. Even though I was cocking my ear towards the town and concentrating hard, I couldn't help realising how famished I was. So I relaxed momentarily, nibbling at some hard bread crusts. April dew crept through my uniform and my limbs felt stiff and numb. I was a broken man, tired, and had to muster all my energy to prevent my eyes from closing. It seemed I was sitting underneath a lead bell without even the tiniest crack through which to escape. Deep slumber allowing

Marshal Ivan Koniev, commander of the 1st Ukrainian Front in the final Soviet advance on Berlin and great rival to Zhukov

me to lose myself in dreams of freedom and oblivion would have been a blessing.

Looking up at the sky, I was struck how the stars above were untouched by the misery of our world; they were, I thought sadly, the same as those shining down on my home town far away. In this mad world one could only hope for help to come from on high. I thought about my parents far away. Surely they were sick with worry about me. Were they even aware of the precarious situation I found myself in at this bleak hour? Angry at myself for being so morose, I quickly pulled myself together. Death hovered at every turn. It was important I focus on the moment.

I plucked some blades of grass from the ground, shoved them into my mouth and, chewing on them, tried to ease my tension.

Somewhere a bird rustled in the bushes . . . instantly I jerked. Calm then set in until dawn 28 April . . . when a thunderous cannonade shook the earth, shattering the silence. The artillery was preparing for our assault. Shells whizzing above our heads peppered the Russian positions with shrapnel; mortar bombs rained down in front of us. The air was filled with a roaring noise – to me it seemed the world was coming to an end. Suddenly there was a whirring and whistling at the southern limits of the town. A stack of Russian ammunition must have exploded. Tongues of bright yellow flame shot upwards like dragon fire, followed by billowing smoke spreading across the town. German artillery increased its fire to hurricane level and the earth shook underneath us as if pummelled by giant fists.

Then suddenly it was time. The order whispered from one foxhole to the other urged us into action. 'Prepare to advance!' With trembling fingers I checked my kit. Was the helmet sitting tight? Was my bayonet in place? Were my hand grenades tucked into my belt? My shovel . . . where was it? I could hear the metal clicking of safety catches. Then, abruptly, the firing stopped . . . Houses were aglow, yellowish-red clouds lay heavy over the rooftops before spiralling upwards like corkscrews.

The infantry would surely attack any moment now, I swallowed hard and ground my teeth. I made sure I had a good strong stance, and pushing back against this I got ready to dart forwards. A coloured flare shot up, the signal for us to start the attack. A terrible day was about to begin. Deployed in extended battle formation we hurried forwards towards the town. Shouted orders kept telling us to cover the soldier next to us. We came ever closer to Halbe. I feared death would crush me at any moment or that I would be horribly mutilated. Luckily the return fire was weak. But then, all of a sudden, the Russians woke up. Concentrated infantry fire hailed down. Though ordered to fan

Yet more Red Army units head for the woods around Märkisch Buchholz and Halbe, closing in on the German troops passing through the area during their frantic retreat.

General of Armoured Troops Walter Wenck commanded Twelfth Army, charged with holding open a possible escape route from the Halbe encirclement into American captivity for their comrades in Ninth Army.

out, we were bunched so thickly that the bullets could hardly fail to hit their targets. Swept by machine-gun fire, comrades sank to the ground. Anti-tank gunners indiscriminately fired at our men who crumpled into a heap of tumbling corpses like flaming torches. Artillery rounds detonated in front us, behind us mud sprayed into the air. Shells burst in glowing white flashes; thick dark smoke whirled around. The lad next to me howled, screamed and fell into the mud as if struck by lightning.

One long and hoarse 'Hurrah' escaped our throats. Bullets whistled past me. Shots ricocheted. Then I heard the unsettling howling sound of a Stalin's Organ rocket* ripping a hole near me blowing men into mounds of bloody corpses. Clothes shredded, dangling body parts, faces dug into the earth, fists clutching a clump of dirt. Some actually tried to lift themselves up and stumbled forwards a step, but then buckled and with flailing arms slumped down. Those who survived sought protection under the dead bodies of their fallen comrades.

---

* Stalin's Organ was the German nickname for Soviet Katyusha rocket artillery equipment.

Urging us on, our company commander charged forwards. There was to be no stopping, no catching one's breath. He was firing constantly himself as enemy bullets smacked down like in a hailstorm. Then I saw him push up his arms, sway and fall. A huge splinter had penetrated through his helmet and skull. An energetic sergeant took over and roared, 'All of you, with me!' The break-through continued.

Above us, night was fading into day. Shells detonated all around us, splinters raining down like lava. We threw ourselves to the ground, scrambled to our feet seconds later, relentlessly storming ahead straight towards the muzzle flashes. Jumping forwards in spurts, taking cover, getting forwards a little at a time, managing first ten metres, then slowing down to five. Dead comrades were instantly buried in the sand thrown up by the detonating shells.

A howling, then a crashing. Bullets whipped past from all directions. A thudding of mortars, a rattling of machine guns, spitting fire – mayhem. Suddenly I felt a burning pain in my left leg. Hobbling, I stumbled on, grimly clenching my teeth. A splinter, at the end of its course, must have hit me and embedded itself in my flesh. Blood was running down my shin and dripping to the ground. No time to think. The battle became more vicious still, the firing more ferocious. The crashing and banging and the cracking bullets didn't seem to stop. We fired like mad. At long last we climbed over the embankment on the Berlin–Cottbus rail line, taking cover wherever we could, in ditches, behind tree trunks and in the shrubbery.

We had reached the edge of Halbe. Bullets were flying from roof tops, shop fronts and hatchways. It was an inferno with artillery shells detonating outside one window and mortar bombs exploding by another. Machine-gun tracer bullets illuminated the early morning sky with their blue-whitish jets of flame setting the tightly packed buildings ablaze. Each house was a fortress, spewing ruin and death.

Somewhere concentrated fire from Panzerfausts reverberated along with the barking of a Panzerschreck. German mortar bombs and anti-tank rockets went off constantly. Once again, my mind needed to escape. But where to? I didn't care, as long as I could flee this hellish trap.

How Long Will our House Stay Standing?

Willi Haenecke, ex-mayor of Halbe

The next morning, I explained to the couple that, come what may, I would want to join my family who had found refuge in the Wagner family's cellar. Escape, I had realised, was not viable. If my fate was death, then it should be amongst family. So I left where I was and when I crawled down into the Wagner cellar, everyone there approved of my decision. My wife and my son Eberhard above all were overjoyed. Now we were together, whatever came our way, we would be prepared and face it as a family.

Night fell ... There was artillery fire from the south, from Teurow or Oderin. There was fierce shelling nearby. By that time, we had left the building and were camped outside, lying on the ground. Then we heard a commotion from the street, a mixed crowds of troops and civilians broke out in the direction of Löpten; shouted orders were drowned out by the engine noise of passing vehicles. Suddenly a shell exploded in the middle of the street, ripping into the column of soldiers. We couldn't see exactly where it was but I think it was near the asylum. The following day we would learn that there were eight dead and several wounded.

Germany's standard infantry anti-tank weapons were the Panzerschreck (*left*), a copy of the American bazooka, and the Panzerfaust, a single-shot weapon with a disposable launch tube.

The reader might well ask why didn't we Haeneckes stay in our own home? Why did we escape to old Wagner's house near the riverbank? The reason was simple: we figured it was too dangerous to remain in the Lindenstrasse – seeing as it was the main road, cutting through from east to west. A retreating army would be forced to take it. The enemy would not hesitate to blast the army, albeit already defeated, and use their air force too. They would have no compunction about strafing and bombing.

In addition, we had to consider the likelihood of street fighting and we certainly had an inkling of what that entailed from having

An die Bevölkerung von Berlin

Berlin ist eingekesselt!

Die Rote Armee hat einen festen Ring um die Stadt gelegt. Dieser Ring wird unter den Schlägen der Roten Armee immer enger. Bei der katastrophalen Lage der deutschen Truppen an den anderen Frontabschnitten wäre es geradezu töricht, an eine Hilfe für das eingeschlossene Berlin zu glauben.

Die Reste der im Raum von Frankfurt a. O. zerschlagenen deutschen Divisionen sind im Raum südlich Beeskow eingeschlossen und strecken zu Tausenden die Waffen. Die untere Oder wurde auf breiter Front überschritten. Stettin ist besetzt. Hier sind die Russen 30 km über Stettin hinausgestoßen. Gleichzeitig haben andere Sowjettruppen den Hohenzollernkanal überschritten. An der Elbe vereinigten sich Sowjettruppen an mehreren Stellen mit den Amerikanern. Der kleine, bis jetzt noch unbesetzte Teil Deutschlands ist somit in zwei Stücke aufgespalten.

Gleichzeitig hat die Rote Armee nie dagewesene Kräfte an Berlin herangeführt: Zehntausende schwerer Geschütze und Salvengeschütze, Tausende von Bombern und Panzern. Das Schicksal Berlins ist besiegelt. Nichts wird die Rote Armee aufhalten können.

Alle Versuche, die Stadt zu verteidigen, sind vollständig zwecklos.

Bei einer solch erdrückenden Übermacht der Roten Armee wird weiterer Widerstand nur zur vollen Zerstörung dessen führen, was noch in der Stadt verblieben ist. Der Versuch, den Kampf in die Länge zu ziehen, wird zu einer schrecklichen Hungersnot, zu Seuchen und zu dem Tod Zehntausender friedlicher Einwohner führen. Uns ist bekannt, daß Ihr schon jetzt hungert, daß es Euch an Wasser und Licht mangelt. Jeder vernünftige Führer würde sich in einer solchen Lage zu sofortiger Kapitulation entschließen, um die Stadt und das Leben der Bevölkerung, Frauen und Kinder, zu retten.

Doch die verbrecherische Hitlerführung tut das Gegenteil. Sie ruft Euch zum Widerstand auf. Die unverschämte Goebbelspropa-

'Berlin is Encircled': the headine on an aerial propaganda leaflet dropped to some of the German troops still holding out. The message is simply 'Nothing can stop the Red Army.'

34

watched newsreels earlier in the war. It would have been sheer madness to remain at home and, as it turned out, what we feared might happen did happen – but never could we have imagined the extent of the severe mauling, the gruesome scenes we were to witness.

The horrors that unfolded in Halbe were far beyond what this town had ever experienced in its history.

Here are the names of those occupying the house at the river: Herr Wagner and his wife, his grandson Paulus with his wife, and a niece with her child, the wife of our doctor with her two children and four of us Haeneckes. We had barricaded the windows both outside and inside by blocking them with mattresses, not a moment too soon as the battle in Halbe had begun. There's definitely an advantage, it has to be said, in not knowing what's in store for you.

Vicious fighting continued unabated for days. We could tell the house had been hit when the walls and floors reverberated and shook under the impact and that would happen again and again. As we all crouched down in the cellar, chunks of plaster broke off from the ceiling and made us wonder in silence how long the basement roof would hold. When there was a temporary lull in the shelling, I climbed upstairs to take a look at the devastation. Walls had crumbled or been ripped into, with holes measuring 1.5 metres in diameter.

I owned a pair of binoculars and could thus observe what was going on outside. I could see soldiers desperately breaking away, taking the path across our field, towards the river. I saw aircraft striking from above at those fleeing, with planes diving so low our men could surely have picked the enemy off in their cockpits with single shots, but no one in our dismal line-up had any energy left. In our town, houses and vehicles had disappeared in clouds of dust and fire.

Once, walking into the kitchen, I came upon foreign soldiers. They were Hiwis, members of the Vlasov army,* Russians who had fought on our side. Using their bayonets as tin openers, they wolfed down some food before disappearing into the night. Tea for the little ones was made on a one-flame spirit stove but we refrained from using the ordinary stove as the smoke might attract attention. In the grounds next to us stood a battery whose barrage of firing didn't cease, and yet we still managed to sleep, such was our exhaustion.

The battle in Halbe lasted for days. Who was holding the town? Ownership must have changed umpteen times. Yes, of course, fear was gnawing away at our nerves and food ran low, but this, strangely, wasn't our main concern. Everyone was deeply worried about only one thing: would the house withstand the pounding.

Ambush at Halbe

Grenadier Martin Kleint, Panzergrenadier Division 'Kurmark'

We survivors of Panzergrenadier Division 'Kurmark' were armoured infantrymen deployed with the Tigers. After joining SS units in Lietzen, we fought alongside them. That gave us the advantage of being attached to an elite unit where each soldier could trust the other. I was sat relatively safely in my seat on the fourth tank, my machine gun ready. Each tank resembled a colony of ants weaving its way forwards.

At the beginning it all went well. We had no idea which route we were following and yet again we were kept totally in the dark as to where our enemy was positioned and when we would have

---

* Andrei Vlasov was a Red Army general who, after capture, raised an anti-Soviet force to fight alongside the Germans. They saw little action.

The heaviest Soviet battle tank in action at Halbe, the Josef Stalin 2, counterpart of the German Tiger II, a number of which served with Ninth Army and led various of the break-through attempts.

contact with him. In fact, we had no clue about anything, but were simply hoping that our steel vehicles would carry us west, allowing us at the very least not to have to continue our trek on foot. Generally, once atop these tanks, we felt powerful and no longer inferior to the Russians . . .

For a while I was fine, holding on to the turret, but my machine gun then somehow slipped and with our tank brushing against the trees, its muzzle got caught in one of the branches. I lost my balance and had to leap off. This wasn't ideal, what with the tank convoy practically wheel to wheel. The next tank threatened to roll over me – but thankfully both I and my machine gun survived this incident unharmed. I ran after my tank, stretched my hand clutching the machine gun upwards, steadied myself on the steel hawser fitted to the rear of the tank and clung on to an iron clip installed next to the track to get back on.

In the meantime, night had fallen and it had stopped raining – fortunately, as it put an end to us getting soaked through. Anti-tank shelling, too, had died down and our journey continued without further incident. We reached a paved road, allowing us to advance more swiftly, crossed a train track and read the sign saying 'Halbe'. Swerving around the corner, we rolled into the town when suddenly there was a mammoth anti-tank salvo targeting us from all directions. Within minutes three tanks had burst into flames. Crews squeezed themselves out of their narrow hatches completely wrapped in flames. The second tank exploded, my machine gun fell out of my grasp and I sought cover behind a tree.

Then an artillery barrage started. Flares shot into the air, shots whipped through the darkness, the rest of our tanks reversed. Eventually . . . total silence. All of a sudden someone yelled: 'Don't shoot, these are our comrades!' That was followed by a babble of voices all shouting over each other. Masses of soldiers lurched forwards into the middle of the town. At that moment we came under ferocious attack from the surrounding houses and our group ended up staggering through the town under heavy and accurate fire. Against the glare of burning armoured vehicles, we became a splendid target. The only shelter came from the trees at the sides of the street. Then, from the other western side of the road we were harassed by Soviet anti-tank guns or tanks.

In the panic and chaos we couldn't distinguish one officer from the next, or make any sense of the orders being given. We had no maps, no plan – we didn't have the faintest idea of how to break out of this pocket. At long last the voice of a Feldwebel cut through the din: 'Machine guns and Panzerfausts, to the front!' A crew member of a tank slowly swinging around flung an ammunition belt in my direction and, dashing past a burning tank, I returned to the protection of the shrubbery.

Now several of us blasted at houses and windows with our machine guns and Panzerfausts. With our fire as cover, others stormed a house on the left side of the road. Dull thuds of our hand-grenades exploding cleared the entry into the building where at long last we found sufficient protection to patch up the injured. Heaps of them were strewn all over the road, wailing, moaning, screaming out in pain. We gathered them up as best we could and carried them into the cellar.

It was an inferno, a ghastly scene of brutality with pools of blood everywhere. The night was pierced by the desperate screams of dying men mixed with the reverberations of countless bombs hailing down and detonating. Aglow with the burning of our own tanks, the town trembled with the rattling of machine guns and shells crashing down. The Russian gunfire was accurate. We were determined to recover one of our comrades who had lost a leg in the shooting and was desperately attempting to claw his way off the street which was all the time being sprayed by enemy fire. We could only watch as one of our own tanks rolled over him literally crushing him to a pulp.

An Army medic turned up in the cellar; taking over from us he bandaged the injured and dressed wounds whilst urging us to move on. 'Get away, find protection, I'll stay here and hand over the wounded to the Russians.' Numb, we shook his hand and took the rear exit of the building, which was shielded from the heavy street shelling. Only once we had reached the edge of the forest did we breathe a sigh of relief.

Who would have thought that this was the exact spot where later on a cemetery for the soldiers killed in Halbe would be created – rows upon rows of graves for over 20,000 of our comrades who had fallen in a few days of ferocious fighting in this 'break-through' battle.

Break-Through Day

Oberscharführer Paul Greinke, Waffen-SS

Wouldn't you know it, but just short of Halbe I actually came face-to-face with my old commander, SS Obergruppenführer Matthias Kleinheisterkamp. On the day of our break-through masses of soldiers had piled up behind columns of vehicles. Intermittently we could hear the announcement bellowed over megaphones: 'Attention! General von Rohde is leading our combat group!'

At that same moment a half-track drove past me and my comrade, a Rottenführer. We could see Kleinheisterkamp standing erect next to his driver who was sat low down in his hatch. Urging us onward he shouted: 'Attention! Today is the day of our break-through – and we will prevail!' Until then I had only ever known this old commander by name as the leader of the 3rd Battalion, SS Regiment 'Deutschland'.

Barely able to breathe for being squeezed from all sides by Landsers pressing forwards and having absolutely no desire to end up at the rear of this formation, I screamed over to my comrade: 'Let's get moving to the front. Let's do anything to get out of this mess!' With the vehicles tangled in one huge traffic jam it was fairly easy to push our way forwards on foot and when dusk fell, there we were at the front. The assault on Halbe had commenced.

All hell broke loose the minute we passed the entrance gates to the sawmill and crossed the rail-tracks. Ivan was now occupying

Tagesmeldung

OKH

In die Durchbruchslücke zwischen dem beiderseits Schöneiche stehen-
den LVI.Pz.Korps und der Südfront CI.A.K. führte der Feind starke
Panzer- und Infanterie-Kräfte nach. Im Vorstoß nach Westen und
Nordwesten aus dem Raum Bernau haben Panzerspitzen Wandlitz und We-
sickendorf erreicht. CI.A.K. wurde in schweren Kämpfen gegen Ebers-
walde und westlich zurückgeworfen.

Aus dem Raum Werneuchen nach Süden und Südwesten angreifend, steht
Feind im Angriff auf die nordostwärtigen Vororte der Reichshauptstadt. Er hat hier gegen den äußeren Verteidigungsring zwischen
Dahlw. Hoppegarten - Schildow mit Infanterie, Artillerie und Panz
kräften aufgeschlossen.

LVI.Pz.Korps hat sich auf die äußere Befestigungslinie mit rechte
Flügel Ostrand Gr. Müggelsee, mit linkem Flügel westlich Dahlw.
Hoppegarten zurückgekämpft.

Gegen die Nordfront des XI.SS-Pz.Korps griff der Feind den ganzen
Tag über mit starken Kräften an und drängte das Korps in die all-
gemeine Linie Petershagen - Falkenhagen - Haselfelde - Steinhöfel -
Fürstenwalde zurück.

Durch das Hereinführen starker Feindkräfte von Norden in den Raum
westlich Fürstenwalde bereitet sich im Zusammenhang mit den aus de
Raum Luckau - Lübben nach Norden und Nordwesten vordringenden Fein
die Einkesselung der Masse 9.Armee vor.

Südlich Berlin warf Feind eigene schwache Sicherungskräfte nach Nor
in die Linie Luckenwalde - Königswusterhausen zurück und brach in d
Abendstunden erneut mehrfach in die aufgebaute Sicherungslinie ein.
Feind hat Treuenbrietzen genommen und greift nach Westen weiter an.

Bei 3.Panzerarmee weitete der Feind durch das Nachgeben der Pol.Bri.
1 seinen Brückenkopf beiderseits der Reichsautobahn aus. Durch sof. t
eingeleitete Gegenangriffe gelang es, diesen Brückenkopf auf die Li
Wilhelmshöhe - Ostrand Hohenzahden - Südostrand Kurow zusammenzudr

A German Army High Command situation report for 21 April notes how
Ninth Army is in danger of being encircled from the south.

A modern photograph of the station at Bad Saarow Pieskow, for a time during the fighting the location of Ninth Army headquarters.

the town. Fierce fire from cellar and loft hatches prevented us from penetrating the rows of houses. Tanks and assault guns bombarded the place, firing again and again as if there literally was no tomorrow. Gutters and streets were gushing with blood. Such was the confusion that Landsers would at times be firing into our own ranks. That was all we needed. Zig-zagging forwards, taking cover by pressing myself into an alcove of a protruding wall, I waved to my comrades to follow me. Countless corpses, both Russian and German, were strewn all over the streets. Once, darting for cover, I slipped on the entrails of a dead soldier and by the time I had scrambled to my feet, I had lost track of my Rottenführer.

At that moment the noise of an approaching tank destroyer urged me into action, and I immediately knew full well what the intentions of the crew were. As I hurled myself onto its hull I realised that one of the crew members might assume I was an Ivan and yelled into the open hatch that I was one of their own. Fortunately, it all worked out. Smashing past the rows of houses which were now engulfed in clouds of smoke and fire, the tank wheeled full throttle onto a forest path close to the Autobahn.

Passing a group of refugees, old people and children, we tore into a turning to join the road. Just then we were targeted by shells of all calibres plunging through the treetops with massive explosions. The blazing inferno was also pierced by the barking of anti-tank guns. It felt like regiments of artillery were firing flat out on all the approaches to the bridge and at the bridge itself. An old refugee woman fell to the ground, arms spread wide. I wanted to run to her aid, but was prevented by a shell hitting just about the same spot – completely shredding the woman. Nothing of her was left.

I was still clinging to the hull of the Hetzer tank destroyer, hardly even noticing that a bullet had hit me in the hand and shattered the butt of my gun. Horrified, I screamed into the hatch for the driver to make a dash for it. 'Go, go,' I yelled, 'Right now!' That's when I heard someone else screaming that General Rohde was injured. 'His tank is alight!' Our Hetzer swerved, brushing past the burning wreck of General Rohde's tank. Our left track caught the edge of the deck of the bridge and I realised we were about to overturn. My pulse racing, I jumped off and hastily crossed the bridge while bombarded by a torrent of targeted gunfire . . . Against all odds I reached the other side.

An order for Ninth Army to retreat from the commander of Army Group Vistula, Colonel-General Heinrici, widely regarded as the German Army's leading defensive tactician.

Close-Quarter Engagement in the Pocket

Marcel Staar, Luxembourg citizen drafted into the Wehrmacht

Picking our way carefully to the rear of the rows of buildings and ducking instinctively when we heard a particularly large thump or the hissing sound of shells flying in our direction, we were aiming to penetrate the Russian defence line. A gaping hole in one particular house with its unhinged door dangling from its frame caught our attention. Cautiously, with my rifle at the ready, I inched forwards, keeping stopping to listen. I was on high alert, heart pounding. Danger, evil and insidious, threatened us from every corner. But nothing stirred. Carefully, eyes darting in all directions, I moved further inwards and stumbled across a dead Russian soldier – horribly mutilated and lying in the middle of a thick puddle of blood. His cheeks were waxen, lips apart and his teeth seemed to gleam out at me. I wanted to turn my head away but the dead man's gaze transfixed me.

Gulping down my revulsion, I took one long leap over the corpse and landed in the living room. Cupboards, their doors flung open, must have been emptied hastily. The table was still set, plates were covered in heaps of dust and dirt. Empty beer and liqueur bottles were strewn over the floor. I crunched through the room with my heavy boots crushing porcelain and glass beneath my soles. But I was more hungry than repulsed and, drawn to the full table, I lunged across only to trip over two legs sticking out from underneath the toppled sofa. His mud-yellowish uniform gave him away: a Russian. Nauseous to the core, I nevertheless reached over to the table, grabbing hold of a full beer bottle. I was just about to take a good long swig but caught myself in time and reprimanded myself, 'Be on the look-out and under no circumstances allow yourself to lose control!' Dropping the

A 280-mm Soviet heavy mortar in action in the Brandenburg woods. Weapons of this type used by the 1st Belorussian Front are believed to have been the heaviest Soviet guns employed in the Battle for Berlin.

bottle to the floor I seized on the roast, tore off a huge chunk and wolfed it down. The gritty feel of my teeth crunching sand didn't much bother me and it certainly calmed my nerves. But it didn't prevent me bounding up the narrow wooden staircase to the loft.

I just couldn't help it – I had to get my bearings and a sense of where I'd landed. Entering a bedroom, I confronted a terrifying scene of wanton demolition, pillage and murder. Shell hits had smashed huge holes in one of the concrete walls and the blast must have driven another wall inwards. Drawers and shelves had been swept bare; stuff was scattered across the floor. Even up here, I saw shattered limbs and torn-open bodies, burn wounds shimmering in the dark. Ripped curtains fluttered aimlessly in the draft and I could still hear gun shots reverberating in the hollow scaffolding of what once was a home. Machine-gun salvos hammered the town relentlessly, hand-grenades whipped across the street exploding in doorways and cellar entrances. In between there were pistol shots.

Pressed into a window corner, I risked shooting a glance outside onto the road. A shiver ran down my spine. An unbelievably violent and brutal slaughter was happening under my very eyes. Russian soldiers piled out of the house opposite and with cold steel furiously stabbed anyone in their way. The groaning of the wounded and the dying was drowned out by those howling in pain and the general din of the battle. Horses galloped around as if beset by furies, dragging their riders behind them, their boots still stuck in the stirrups. Hit by a bullet, animals reared up and then, fighting their final battle, collapsed. I couldn't actually take it all in. My knees buckled but I got downstairs. Where were my comrades? Plunged into this dreadful and packed pocket, I was desperate to catch up with them.

I climbed into the cellar next door where I heard some voices. Holding my breath, I tried to make out whether they were Germans or Russians. Some tense moments ticked by. But then I heard it quite clearly: 'Ivan is retreating!' I clattered up the stony cellar stairs and stared straight into someone's pistol muzzle. When my 'opponent' recognised a comrade, he lowered his arm immediately. The men who were gathered here indeed belonged to my squad and I was jubilant. What luck! 'And here to top it all off, we have our Feldwebel!' I exclaimed, recognising him immediately, though he was crouched down in an alcove near the window scanning the street below him with his binoculars.

Fully kitted up, I threw myself to the ground alongside some other soldiers. My mate next to me whispered that the Feldwebel was desperately trying to locate a machine gun which had been causing huge casualties. This explanation had scarcely been given when the Feldwebel suddenly exclaimed that he had found the source. He winked at his Obergefreiter as we unconsciously held our breath . . . and then there was a dull thud . . . huge clouds of brick dust and mortar whirled through the room and a wide gaping hole stared down on us from a gable wall. The Russian machine-gunner had vanished into thin air. A Panzerfaust had done its work.

Finally, the noise of the fighting around us ebbed away. The Russians had obviously retreated. Nonetheless, each one of us moved out of the house slowly and extremely cautiously. We were ordered to push forwards to the train station and clear the surrounding fields of enemy forces. 'Boy,' the Feldwebel turned to me, 'till now, we've been damn lucky. But there's no way we can hold this town until the end.'

Our company now reduced to a strength of six men, we followed him, past the badly damaged church and school, guns at the ready and without losing sight of the opposite side of the road. At every step we stumbled across dead soldiers of the two nations – plus civilians, women, children, old people – prostrate on the ground, or in heaps a metre high. The roads were strewn with overturned vehicles, either shot up or destroyed. Weapons had been blown up, goods and belongings trampled.

Turning slightly right at the fork of Hauptstrasse and Kirch-strasse we were able to scan the area around the train station. In front of us was a scene of devastation. Flames of the burning furniture factory still leapt into the air, illuminating the ruins in a spooky light. Next to it was the station master's lodge and to its side the red and white signs of the rail crossing rising up to the sky like two fingers warning of impending disaster. Crossing the tracks, which were carpeted in corpses, we passed an unserviceable signal box. The white sign fastened to the red brick station building had the black letters HALBE written on it. On the tracks stood burnt-out freight wagons and exploded railway engines. Next to them were damaged assault guns and

An order from General Krebs of the Army High Command adjusting
the boundary between Ninth Army and Army Group Centre
on its right flank.

A modern view of the remains of a trench system near Müllrose. The area was likely heavily wooded in 1945 though the trees in the photograph are clearly of more recent growth.

smashed staff cars. Two demolished tanks were still burning – two flaming torches in a garden.

Suddenly I heard a short sharp bang. It was our Feldwebel. He had headed our column and been hit by a bullet going straight to his heart. He keeled over. Dead. A stream of blood covered his back in red. Dumbfounded we stood still for just a second but then immediately threw ourselves to the ground. An Unteroffizier who had come running to help the Feldwebel collapsed without making a sound. A bullet had hit his head, entering just above his nose.

Somebody was yelling: 'Sniper!' Three men lay there as if paralysed. One Gefreiter, taking his life in his hands, slid off the road and disappeared. The rest of us, jittering, were too stunned to think. Should we leap up – should we hide in a hollow? Where? Another hissing sound of a bullet. Shortly, though, the Gefreiter returned. 'Get yourself up, you lame ducks,' he snapped. With one hand grenade he had wiped the sniper off the face of this earth. Crouching low we made a dash to the station building.

Staggering and slipping over the wounded, dying and dead soldiers and civilians, we could still hear the sound of battle coming from the surrounding forests, especially the woodland to the west. We knew that heavy fighting was taking its toll. The break-through, we gathered, had been successful. Then, as if he had been dropped from the sky, our Stabsfeldwebel stood at the station building to welcome us.

Though by then the number of us dolts could be counted on the fingers of one hand, he nevertheless was overjoyed to have us join his band. He had been ordered to assemble those remaining from his battalion and ensure all transport routes covering the Märkisch Buchholz–Halbe–Teupitz and the Hammer forestry area remained open, even beyond the brick factory right up to the Halbe train station. The reason was to keep a break-out route open for those enclosed in the pocket, preferably along the train tracks.

From the position to which I had been assigned I had a clear field of vision with the train tracks crossing in front of me. Endless streams of military personnel, rearguards and refugees, frail civilian men and women surged forwards, disorientated and desperate, past vehicles still aglow, past dead horses and grotesquely disfigured corpses. Anxious, frightened people screamed both at each other and at no one in particular, terror in their eyes. You could hear tank tracks screeching, cars honking and cyclists ringing their bells. Women pushed prams while small children clung to their dresses, old men tottered forwards pulling behind them carts heaped with all kinds of household goods and jamming the path. Wounded, exhausted soldiers leaning on crutches or with an arm in a sling limped painfully through the boggy terrain. With every Russian artillery salvo making yet more craters in the landscape, panic broke out then turned into mortal fear when the Red ground-attack aircraft flew dive-bombing raids leaving beneath them raging destruction. I too was terrified.

What an earth did this insane break-through battle being fought by the Ninth Army actually have to do with me, a simple guy from Luxembourg who had been forced into the Wehrmacht against both his and his parents' will? What could help save me from this inferno? Aware that I could be ordered to report for action at any moment, I had to find a cunning strategy . . . and fast. A possible order to seal off an enemy penetration or even embark on a counter-attack would spell certain death for me, I knew that much.

Desperate, I swiftly slit apart the left arm of my jacket with my bayonet, rolled up my shirt sleeve and plunged the field dressing that I carried on me into a fresh puddle of blood before bandaging

A casualty report from Ninth Army to Army Group Vistula.

my arm. This made me 'freshly wounded'. Having accomplished my ruse and with the little energy I had left, I swung myself up onto the front wing of a passing ambulance heading to the Hauptstrasse despite the protestations of the driver who railed against his vehicle being overloaded. It was the only free spot.

Not able to hold on properly, I pressed against the radiator guard so as not to slip off.

Battalion Blocked – Penetration Impossible

Oberscharführer Ernst Streng, 502nd Heavy Tank Battalion

With a clear view south to Halbe, at last light we roll past a large timber yard and sawmill towards the Halbe station, undisturbed by the enemy.

Our tank comes to a halt just in front of the railway crossing and literally thousands of infantry stream past us. Reconnaissance reports: 300 metres ahead of us, in the middle of a row of houses fronting the town at the exit route towards the Autobahn, anti-tank obstacles. No shot has yet been fired. As night falls, a few isolated fires flicker and lighten up the darkness setting in.

I glance down from my tank which is winding its way through mounds of scrap metal, burnt-out trucks and tractors and wrecked horse-drawn carts and squashed staff cars. Columns of soldiers and civilians piled up against each other are barely able to advance: a traffic jam of huge proportions has developed and movement is reduced to a crawl. Everyone is clamouring to join the break-through spearheaded by the tanks, as if their armour was a certain guarantee of protection and safety. Amongst the throngs of human misery left over from what were once fighting divisions you see ambulatory wounded, with sticks in hand, hobbling along, their torsos bent over. And even those whose heads have been bandaged but can still walk upright seem despondent. A flat expression in their eyes says enough; lips firmly pressed together, they still believe that somewhere and at some point this march will penetrate the Russian encirclement and lead to freedom. That's their hope. This is the hope that drives them on and momentarily lets them forget all pain and hardship.

The general issues his orders. Fall in and break through! Clear a way through Halbe and then make for the Autobahn. Kuhnke thrusts forwards, over the railway crossing, keeping to the right and heading for a road flanked by trees on either side. The leading tank platoon and my own crew follow.

It is the most frightful sight: tanks are lined up nose to tail and soldiers pressed against each other, generals and ordinary soldiers all packed together, rifles or sub-machine guns in their hands . . . The throng shoves up the street and then, like a lava flow, oozes out in between the buildings and back gardens.

A former German defensive bunker near the River Schlaube.

A post-war view of the station buildings at Scharmützelsee, site of
Ninth Army headquarters at the start of the cauldron battle.

Walls shake, sharp-edged glass splinters fall out of window
frames and the tanks grind their way through the town. All of a
sudden, right in front of us, the first shells explode, sending fragments hissing and howling; we hear the dry crack of machine
guns and countless bombs hailing down. There is a brief pause in
the firing and the crowd seems confused. Seconds later soldiers
thrust forwards under the protection of the tanks, cheering
loudly. Then darkness finally falls and with it panic breaks out.
Everyone seeks cover behind the tanks, or beside the buildings.
The Russians shell us continuously.

After some hundred metres the column comes to a standstill.
Kuhnke radios that he has got to about 30 metres short of the
anti-tank barrier and is asking for infantry support. I don't have

a clear view of the blockade. In the meantime, the streets are choked with trucks and exploding shells. Soldiers and civilians jam themselves in between the trees lining Angerstrasse which is thirty metres wide. I turn off to the right in order to orientate myself. Enemy shells relentlessly pound the surrounding buildings and the Lindenstrasse.

Smoke billowing from the buildings covers the battleground, tongues of bright flame leap skywards. Lofts are alight, blazing fires illuminating the ghostly night. The murderous attacks reach a crescendo and total chaos follows: the break-through of the Ninth Army has reached its climax. What angers us tank crews most is the fact that due to the streets overspilling with people and armament we are prevented from deploying our 8.8 centimetre anti-tank guns effectively. In front of us, on the narrowest frontage imaginable, a swirling fight rages: close combat in between the buildings and back gardens. Despite, or rather because of, both sides blasting away furiously, from all angles, there is no chance of advancing, no gaining space for those of us on the attack. Wedged between other tanks, our vehicles – some with, others now without their drivers – are halted and helpless, amongst them the dead, the wounded, the screams for medical orderlies.

Kuhnke radios that the assault troops are being blocked. Nobody seems to know where Ivan has embedded himself. An assault troop charged with encircling the enemy encounters obstacles. High explosive and phosphorus shells burst with glowing white splashes, shooting fire everywhere. Now it is getting serious. The infantry are mustering all their courage, but there is no way out. Suddenly my hatch receives a direct hit to the front, and within seconds the vehicle is on fire with a blinding whiteness spraying out. Ott the driver yells through the intercom 'Vehicle on fire' and everyone wrenches open his hatch. I tumble out of the turret head first and hit the road surface hard as my pistol clatters onto the stony ground. Leaping up to make a dash for it, I find that the blast has torn off my helmet. Ott hits the side panel and crushes his ribs. We break away from the tank and flee down the street. Turning around to hurry the crew along, I come to my senses when I see our tank engulfed by flames in the middle of a mess of fallen telegraph poles, rubble, crushed trees and shattered glass, broken tiles. Our tank, a dark mass of burnt metal, is illuminated by the flames blazing from vehicles and rooftops. Yes, I think to myself, we have definitely been hit by an incendiary shell.

I shout for the crew to board a tank, and we climb up on one after the other. My hands are burning from phosphorus splashes. Ott sits in the driver's seat groaning with pain and informing us

Soviet troops come under heavy German fire during fierce forest fighting.

that he is unable to continue – in the middle of all this. But he has to drive – he just has to. The lives of our crew depend on him; we must come through. We no longer have contact with Kuhnke. He doesn't respond to our messages. Damn! What has happened?

Our company leader orders all tanks to reverse and withdraw into a side street. 'Halbe is to be traversed on the east!' This order doesn't come a moment too soon as there is no way to cut through the barrier. I am to withdraw all tanks immediately and clear the street. Kuhnke's lead tank is shelled whilst turning and trying to escape. It bursts apart with a bright flash of flames; the fire threatens to engulf us. A few of the crew bail out. Around us, everyone, crew and vehicles, tries to escape from the hellishly narrow streets. On my right I make out a tank pulling up, it belongs to the 1st Platoon but in the darkness and general chaos I cannot read the number. Then things unfold in front of my eyes. As my neighbouring tank mounts a pavement, its tracks get caught on a heavy truck crashing the cab and the engine underneath its rear with the flaming gases from the exhaust then setting fire to the crushed fuel pipes. Within seconds flames shoot up and envelop both the tank and the heavy truck in a sea of fire. The badly wounded men and the accompanying grenadiers riding on the back and turret of the tank fall like flaming torches to the ground, followed by the crew. And who will care?

I too am forced to withdraw a few metres. Flames jetting out of a nearby tank threaten to engulf me and my vehicle. I see a bright flash of flame shooting up from the direction of the tank barrier with subsequent explosions spraying ammunition over the glowing tank sides in the dark of the night.

After some time has passed I sense that the road behind me has been cleared. Blinded by the surrounding glare of the fire I see tanks reversing, slowly, disappearing in the blackness of the trees. For several minutes the street remains under systematic

A Hetzer tank destroyer unit in the streets of Guben in Brandenburg at the end of March 1945.

tank fire from behind the anti-tank barrier. The battle lasts for what seems like hours after which, towards midnight, the order is received to clear Halbe of the tanks. It is 29 April.

A Dangerous Suggestion

Karl-Heinz Driemel, Halbe

The single map that has so far emerged from those days that outlines the combat operations in Halbe yields important information: the Soviets obviously possessed accurate knowledge of the town and knew all about the anti-tank obstacle at the end of Lindenstrasse. This enabled them to deploy their heavy machine guns, tanks, mortar battalions and their artillery effectively, and do so in such a way that the bottleneck-shaped town became a trap and the site of a lethal ambush. The map shows that the barrier, constructed by German pioneers between Halbe and the narrow pass in Teurow, turned out to be more of a help to their enemies and conveniently provided them with good aiming points for their fire.

Why then and for what reason was the layout of the fateful town of Halbe so completely unknown to the Germans? What might explain why Halbe became a horrific tangled maze for everyone, from the top military commanders down to the lower-ranking officers of both armies including divisional, regimental and countless battalion commanders?

Why were horses and their riders in the same predicament as the columns of refugees, despite having heavy tanks at their disposal? Time and again they'd roll right through the centre of the town. What was the reason? Did no one send reports to the rear with information on what they saw, what was happening

Men of an anti-tank unit moving up to the front. Their half-tracked artillery tractor is well loaded with supplies.

and what horror awaited anybody who tried to get through the town?

I'd like to mention a typical and indeed curious incident that took place near Halbe during those days that might give pause for thought. Now, after decades have passed since these tragic events, inhabitants of Halbe still remember that one of their men, a soldier called Michallek, a truck driver, arrived near Halbe while the battle was in full swing. Some of those who had tried to get through told the waiting troops of the heavy losses suffered in the town and that there was absolutely no chance of going that way. Michallek, thus runs the story, plucked up the courage to approach a bunch of undecided officers gathered around to deliberate their position, and he offered his help. He would, he suggested, lead everyone there around the town. Seeing as Halbe was his home and he was familiar with its geography, he knew that north of Halbe the terrain was not marshy, that there were no water obstacles; he was prepared to lead the way because as far as he could tell they, including the tanks, would all cut through successfully.

Barely able to finish his words, he wished he had bitten his tongue as he was instantly suspected of being a traitor. Indeed, such was the horrified reaction that he had to fear for his life. Fortunately for him, however, his papers indicated Halbe as his place of birth. Nonetheless, the officers of this particular unit were obstinate, so much so that they actually insisted on heading straight into Halbe. Nearly all of them perished, including their leader. On reflection, it all seems jinxed; it stinks of treason Or, it was due to mindless decisions and a total absence of careful thinking, even from those who were tasked to do so.

29 April 1945

Oberscharführer Horst Woycinick, 32nd SS Division
'30th January', diary extract

It must be getting on for 1330 hours. Resembling a swollen grey inchworm, we're marching on a forest lane leading to what will be the break-through battle. All sorts of vehicles, towing trucks, handcarts, and horse-drawn carriages densely pack the narrow road, alongside floods of soldiers and refugees all streaming to an unknown destiny. Moving like confused sheep around and behind armoured vehicles, we hurry along. Each one of us is lost in his own thoughts, grimly determined to break through and out. Suddenly, some random soldier, not sure from which side, fires the first shots and wide-spread shelling follows with machine

American and Soviet troops meeting in a German town in late April 1945 as the end of the war was clearly approaching rapidly.

guns rattling and tracer bullets whistling over us. Everyone with a weapon uses it. It is sheer madness: those marching to the right or the left of the path direct their fire ahead and those trudging on the path point their weapons to the sides.

What's happening? Is this a case of pent-up emotions bursting out or have those bastards from the National Committee for a Free Germany infiltrated our ranks? We could well do without having to worry about them. Comrades crumble to the ground, dead or left lying to die. Vehicles roll over and crush them to a pulp. Those who have escaped are stunned. Speechless at the sight of vast pools of blood around them, their minds are numbed by the horrific screams of pain echoing from all directions.

Among it all there's firing overhead and we hear bullets whistling over the treetops – it all seems like a jungle. My comrades and I know the position: in front of us lies Halbe – a small town.

Crouching low in the shrubbery we hear all kinds of rumours spreading through the ranks. We're worried about one: a four-barrelled anti-aircraft gun is hard at work ahead of our group. And what about us? What are we doing pressed low to the ground on our stomachs staring into empty space? Finally, we understand that all the firing that had come from our column was not a planned attack but the result of soldiers who lacked combat experience and had panicked. At long last, the shelling calms down and we can lift our heads. Quite a number of our lot are no longer able to do so, though, and just as many are wounded. Women and children are wailing. Some among us muster their energy and call on the rest to get ourselves up and continue marching. Gradually the soldiers come to their senses and move on. In close-knit teams they link up with the vehicles rolling along; stumbling and stomping forwards they seem intently focused on an unknown destination ahead of them. The battle noise from the town grows to a crescendo. The column halts briefly, somehow sensing impending doom, then picks up the pace and, fiercely determined, approaches the battle scene. At dawn we arrive just short of Halbe. There is no mistaking what lies before us. May God be with us!

In the meantime, the forest track we have chosen for our advance is being shelled. Heavily. The unsettling howling of Stalin's Organs, the continuous sounds of combat, of frantic firing of artillery pieces, mortars and assault guns. The deafening explosions going off are overwhelming. Just a hundred metres ahead of us loud cheers reverberate through the air, a thousand voices conjure up superiority over the enemy. Defiant and full of courage the mass thrusts forwards and into the small town. My lot are part of it.

A Red Army SU-100 tank destroyer in flames during the fighting in Brandenburg at the end of April 1945.

Shots fired out of destroyed houses and collapsing ruins cause countless fatalities among our group but, after some initial delays, we soldiers of the Ninth Army are masters of the town. It is 2200 hours. The Russians have cleared out. A bit later I bump into my CO, Obersturmbannführer Hoffmann, mercilessly kicking some guys out of the forestry office where they had tried to find shelter.

Once the area is cleansed of the last Russian defenders we return to the street where we hope to meet up with comrades from our unit. No luck. The two of us are just relieved that we're in this together.

A dressing station is set up in the building. Wounded men and women are carried in. We two devour some food and depart. Our destination: west. The scene we behold is something out of a nightmare: the dead are lying on the street and between the houses, heaps and heaps of them, Russians and Germans all mixed up together. Naturally, as we were the attackers, there are way more Germans.

A shot-up Tiger II and a burnt-out Josef Stalin tank block our road. We head south-west towards the Autobahn, marching down a forest path. In the meantime, the day has become sweltering hot with the sun beating down on us and Russian aircraft picking off their targets – armoured vehicles or small groups of men – like hawks their prey. At regular intervals we come across charred remains of our own anti-tank vehicles. There are also quite a few Russian ones. We are approaching Baruth.

All of a sudden we see women taking the lead. We march throughout the day. The heavy rucksack presses into my back dreadfully. The CO and I take a break every five minutes. The

The Soviet forces often sent infantry into action riding on tanks.
Casualties from this tactic were often high but Soviet commanders
deemed these acceptable in return for the mobility gained.

heat exhausts us and we want nothing more than to lie down for a short while and sleep. No, don't give up and don't fall behind and don't lose contact with the break-through column! You have to keep going, keep going. That's what they say! No water to be had in these woodlands. Then again, I don't feel like having a drink. Filthy and bruised, we just drag ourselves forwards and have lost any interest in the pathways and hamlets we cross. Onwards! Onwards! Head west!

At dawn we encounter a big Russian barrier, a formidable obstacle. Vicious fighting erupts and our advance is blocked. It is certain that the Russian fighter aircraft continually overhead have informed their staff of our break-through column and we are now targeted by the American twin-engined types that the USA has supplied to the Russians. There's not much we can do. Of all the things I hate, I hate bombs most. Bomb after bomb. We are literally being carpeted by bombs. I run as fast as my legs will carry me with explosives detonating all around. Trees are sliced apart showering us with splinters and branches. Bodies ripped apart, skins torn loose, a bloody mess left behind.

I remain unscathed. A miracle? I feel around my body to make sure it's true. Then I look around me and see that my CO is alive as well. In the meantime, bombers roar past above our heads only to return, dive down and sweep the area with their fire. They each have four cannons and machine guns – and there are some fifty enemy aircraft. I dash for cover behind a large tree, make myself as thin as possible . . . 'Up yours,' I think, probably too cocksure for my own good. And then the torrential downpour stops as suddenly as it started. My tree trunk has been almost hollowed out by the bullets. The Russians are vastly superior. Our officers are few and far between. Landsers just roam around and swear. And some try to shirk . . .

Women looking on shake their heads. Some of them push themselves forwards, resolute. Equipped with pistols, rifles and sub-machine guns they storm ahead attacking the Russians under a continuous barrage of fire. And lo and behold, we feel re-invigorated and continue our fight. (Later on, I met up with these women. They were awarded Iron Crosses despite the collapse of the battle and our defeat.)

In the meantime, Oberscharführer Oertel has come under our care. Riddled with shrapnel and splinters, he was picked up near a waterhole and then packed into a vehicle. We're inside with him. The two groups of the Ninth Army which have separately forced the penetration are now joined, ordered to overcome

Soviet infantry with a Maxim heavy machine gun firing on a
German-held village.

A Soviet infantryman armed with a Degtyarev light machine gun looks for a better firing position during an engagement.

what is supposedly the final ring of the Russian encirclement, supported by nothing but the last few Tiger II tanks, what is left over from the supply of four-barrelled anti-aircraft guns, a few other tanks and some miscellaneous armoured vehicles. The situation reminds me of what I witnessed – it seems ages ago – at the Mius front in 1943. At that time every last man on our side was deployed to the front and tasked with penetrating the enemy line.

Night is falling. Despite our nerves being on edge we aren't losing sight of our aim: to reach a fortified German front in order to be left in peace and get some sleep, finally sleep, nothing but

AOK. 9 MELDET FOLGENDE BEFOHLENEN MASSNAHMEN :

1) ZURUECKNAHME DER OST - UND NORD - OST FRONT
IN DIE ALLGEMEINE LIENIE BURG- BUTZEN- SCHWIELOCH- SEE-
SPREE IN EINEM ZUGE IN DER NACHT VOM 23. / 24.4.

2.) ROEM 5. ARM. KORPS UEBERNIMMT BEFEHL UEBER SUEDFRONT
VOM RECHTEN FLUEGEL BIS BURG AUSSCHLIESSLICH ,
ROEM5 SS GEB. ARM. KORPS UEBER OSTFRONT BIS KERSDORFER
SCHLEUSSE .-

3.) FREIWERDENDE KRAEFTE: 342. INF. DIV. 1. VERST.
KAMPFGR. 35. SS DIV. (BISHER AN DER OSTFRONT
EINGESETZT) 1. KAMPFGR. BEI ROEM11 SS PANZ. KORPS IN
STAERKE VON 1 BIS 2 RGT. (FESTUNGSBESATZUNG.) ART. NOCH
NICHT ABZUSEHEN ., WIRD NACH GEMELDET.-

4.) FUER ANGRIFFSGRUPPE VORGESEHEN: KAMPFGR. 21. PANZ
DIV. 342. INF. DIV. TEILE 35. SS DIV. 1. GEPANZERTE GRUPPE
(SS AUFKL. ABT. ROEM 5 GEB.) FRUEHESTER BEGINN 25.4.
FRUEH —

Ninth Army's plan on 23 April supposedly combined an intention to go to
the relief of Berlin with the aim of retreating to the Elbe

sleep. But, alas, there's neither the time nor the place to do so. We move out to the start position. Our legs want to give way, but we keep dragging ourselves forwards to the where we need to go. As it's getting on for midnight, all hell breaks loose with all of us yelling at the top of our voices. We break out in a cold sweat but still run forwards with a loud 'Hurrah!' Hundreds of us keel over in this first onslaught. Trampling over mangled bodies towards the railway embankment we charge across, stumble along the Berlin–Dresden train tracks, spot a road running parallel to them and then stagger towards it. We keep heading north. Along the road, our men are taken prisoners. Can this be true? 'Seydlitz-Troops! Traitors. They're being clubbed to death.' One of them, before dying, even manages to ask the question: 'Are you sure that your cause is so much better than ours?' He is killed instantly. It is midnight.

How I Got Through Halbe

Unterscharführer H. Haufschildt

In the early hours of the day of the break-through, it must have been 29 April, we assembled vehicles and tanks of all kinds and we were ready to fight. The distance to the railway crossing would have been some 100 metres. Thousands of soldiers and civilians gathered at the sawmill and the surrounding area, prepared for the thrust on the town. Suddenly the start area was hit by the shells of an artillery bombardment. What then took place is indescribable. It was pure hell. Finally, the order came: 'Tanks, forwards!'

We are part of the vanguard crossing the embankment and pushing into the town. We stop short of an unexpected anti-

The village of Kehrigk, on the road to Märkisch Buchholz from the east, gave the retreating Ninth Army forces a rare opportunity to rest man and machine.

tank barrier at the Teupitz or Baruth exit where we just about have time to catch our breath. Fortunately, our Tiger II holds the T-34s positioned along the barrier line at bay. Very soon, the thirty-metre wide Lindenstrasse is packed with people intent on breaking through with their vehicles. We are joined by six Hetzer tank destroyers and several Panzer IVs – the perfect target for Soviet artillery, as it turns out, who have watched our movements well. Ivan lets a mortar battalion loose to batter the entangled swarms of people.

There is no way the anti-tank barrier can withstand our onslaught, though. Armoured vehicles hammer the right-hand side of the obstacle with high explosive shells then grind the wreckage down with the tank tracks to mush it into the ground.

It is as if a cauldron has burst into flames. Many thrust forwards towards Teupitz. Throngs of people wind their way along the forest track, towards the Autobahn – and Baruth. Unhindered, we reach the other side of the Autobahn. Our column consists of 15–20 vehicles and a total of some 2,000 civilians and soldiers. Approximately 5 kilometres west of the Autobahn we stop just before a field covered in corpses lying side by side, sometimes on top of each other – including some policemen in their green uniforms. We don't count them but there must be around 300. As for ourselves, we know that surrender is out of the question . . .

Taking over the Ninth Army Rearguard

Standartenführer Hans Kempin, last commander
of the '30th January' Division

Busse's most recent headquarters position unknown. We've only been in radio contact. The last message to reach me said something like this: from a rear-guard position I was to take over command of units which were still scattered. 'Consider the situation and then break out of the pocket,' it said, 'deciding whether to head for Berlin or the Elbe.' I received that order during a successful attack carried out by Matthiebe with his battalion.

On receipt of this order, I realised that I had to disengage. I instructed the medical officer in charge to hand over his field hospital to the Russians. I met Obergruppenführer Jeckeln in a clearing of the woods behind the Hammer forestry office. There he was sitting on a tree or tree trunk with heaps of burnt-out vehicles stacked up around him. I also saw a great number of soldiers who were encamped there and who had plainly given up. As I passed Jeckeln he said to me: 'Kempin, that's it, that's the end.' I responded: 'Maybe it is for you, but not for us, not yet.' That's how I remember it. I'd never been able to stomach that man.

I wouldn't be able re-trace my route through Halbe if I had aerial photos as we were caught up in a Russian air attack which totally engulfed us. That might be the reason why we got through . . .

A Supernatural Presence

Gerhard Würth, radio operator, 26th Anti-aircraft Regiment

Our 8.8-cm battery had arrived just short of the Halbe boundary where the firing position assigned to my lot afforded us a decent view. We then fired off our last shells and then grabbed any weapons within our reach . . . machine guns, rifles. We fanned out and thrust forwards, hurrying into the centre of town, which was already ablaze. Under furious anti-tank fire which met us just at the railway tracks, our assault collapsed. There we were, prostrate on the ground, some dead, others wounded but still alive. We were still trying to collect ourselves when another assault squad charged past us, to be hit by a wall of enemy fire. Barely even able to stand, we were being dragged into the howling inferno of a horrific battle.

It was as if we were under a mad spell. Tactics drilled into us minutely during field training were forgotten. Discipline had disappeared. Attracted like moths to a flame we were drawn to the gleaming muzzles of the guns shelling the pocket to a black mass of ruins, destruction and devastation. Those wanting to escape the cauldron, those refusing to die a meaningless death facedown in the mud, those wanting to break away to the west, were

Fernspruch - Fernschreiben - Funkspruch - Blinkspruch

Nachr.-Stelle	Nr.	Befördert				
		an	Tag	Zeit	durch	Rolle
HRIXISS	1200	Ia:		24/4		
		O.Qu				
Vermerke:		Ic/F:				
Angenommen oder aufgenommen						

von	Tag	Zeit	durch
	23.4.	1850	

Abgang	An:		Reservierende Stelle
Tag:			
23.4. 1655			AOK 9
Dringlichkeits-Vermerk			
KR	= AN H. GR. WEICHSEL =		Fernspruch Bericht:

LETZTE MOEGLICHKEIT VERSORGUNGSAUSFUHR FUER

ARMEE DURCH EINBRUCH GRUENAU UNTERBUNDEN , DAMIT F

EINGELEITETE HILFSMASSNAHMEN HINFAELLIG.

VERSORGUNGSZUFUHR DURCH LUFTLANDUNG ODER

ABWURF VON: 1. 30 CBM OTTO 30 TO PIST. PATR. 08

PIST PATR. 43 FUER GEWEHR PATR. FUER MG

5 TO PANZERFAUST, 8 TO 7,5 CM PZ. GR. PAK 40

5 TO 7,5 CM KWK. 40 6 TO 7,5 SPR. GR. KWK 42 5 TO 8,8 CM

SPR. KWK 43 BALDMOEGLICHST ERBETEN .

FLUGPLATZ NORDWESTL. STORKOW (ZWISCHEN RIEPLOS UND

KUMMERSDORF) WIRD DURCH ARMEE LANDEKLAR GEMACHT

ARM.OBKDO. 9 ROEM 1 A ++

2125 EINS HITZIGER HRIX/SS++

Fernspruch Fernschreiben Funkspruch Blinkspruch	Nr.	Von	An	Tag	Zeit	Durchnehmender Offz. Name	Dienst gr.
	380	BUCHSTABENZ. 696					
		SCHLUESSELZT. 2050 ++					

Ninth Army reports its very limited weapon and ammunition stocks to
Army Group Vistula on 23 April.

forced to pass through the eye of the needle, Halbe, this small town that had become hell on earth.

Was there really no other escape route? The average guy didn't even ask himself that question at the end of April seeing as none of us, men, women, children, refugees and soldiers alike, including our officers, knew any better. Plus, none of us had any useful maps to hand. Who the hell knew why these smart generals of ours chose Halbe of all places to be quite literally the final word on this war? What did we Germans actually know about Halbe? We didn't even know whether Halbe was a village or a city. We had no idea of the infrastructure, the direction of the streets, where any of the main buildings were situated. We

The 24 April 1945 edition of the *Berliner Morgenpost* newspaper optimistically proclaims, 'Berlin will never be surrendered to the Soviets – the Führer is with us.'

had no clue about where there might be any bridges. Basically, we were completely ignorant of any details which would have been essential to possess prior to penetrating an area with even the slightest expectation of being successful. Neither within the upper echelons of the army nor further down was there a single person who even had the faintest idea about the place they wanted stormed and, worse still, they had zero knowledge about the anti-tank barriers at the exit points.

These barriers had been set up by German pioneers months before. Some of us had no inkling of their existence until they stood smack in front of them where they were then knocked over . . . dead. Had they been forgotten while, or because, our troops were too busily engaged in skirmishes? Thus, unsuspecting, one by one, we thrust into Halbe, a clueless army headed by a general and some officers. Ivan was the only one who actually reached Halbe fully informed as to what was what, knowing what the hell, in the literal sense, was happening.

How can this be explained? How come he knew the town like the inside of his trouser pocket? How on earth did he find out exactly where the church stood, of where the strategic fixed points were, where we had positioned the two anti-tank barriers? It looked like everyone on the other side, from marshal to private soldier was totally familiar with what he was dealing with. Ivan apparently had precise information on the unique military opportunity that had presented itself: the two rows of red pine logs rammed into the ground with the space in between filled with Märkisch sand – these were clearly marked on Ivan's defence plan. No doubt about it: the enemy knew exactly what to do, when they wanted to target us with their Maxim machine guns.

It happened all at once: shells flying across the awfully narrow streets and exploding all around; bullets hailing down from the church; more firing coming from the edge of the forest, over the

A Red Army SU-85 tank destroyer seen in the tree-lined streets of a
German town in May 1945

hilltops and across the vineyard. Let Fritz do his thing, they must
have thought, let him go ahead and try his luck ... we've got
him in the bag big-time! Yes, indeed, our enemy 'comrade' was
beautifully kitted out for his very last battle against the Ninth
Army.

And so it came to pass. We Fritzes did come on. We
approached in our masses; we practically flooded the area like a
torrent. As if sent by the devil, our men poured out of the forest
straight towards Halbe, and there was Ivan tucked up both inside
the town and around it, not taking his finger off the trigger and
hurling grenades as if there was no tomorrow – bang, crash,
bang, crash. But where was I? Ah, yes ...

After finally reaching the railway crossing, which was carpeted in corpses, we pushed in between the rows of houses and forwards. Shells were bursting to the right and left, at our backs and right in front of us. Ground-attack aircraft struck from above and smoke erupting all around obscured the scene. The town was aglow. It seemed as if everyone was shooting everyone, hand grenades smacked onto pavements, Panzerfaust rockets crashed through window panes. Keeping close to the brick walls, we once again stomped over corpses, past burnt-out buildings, little more than ruins, past wrecked vehicles still smouldering. We stumbled over the injured and turned a blind eye . . . Yes, that was the scene on the Lindenstrasse, the main street of Halbe, on that day. I leapt from a tree trunk down to what was left of a shot-up tank. Then cautiously moving on, I ducked behind some trucks, still inching forwards. I remember slipping over the bloated corpse of a dead horse and then . . . into the front hall of a house to exit swiftly through a hole in the back, landing in a bomb crater where I got entangled in a wrecked horse-drawn wagon. I freed myself and kept painfully stumbling along. I had lost all sense of direction.

The deeper we thrust into the town, the weaker our attack became. Exposed to hours and hours of ferocious Soviet bombardment, we simply lost the will to carry on fighting. With the perimeter of the pocket steadily contracting, our once powerful troops were broken, their fighting power faded and finally disappearing completely. A short distance away from the barrier, now reduced to pulp and splinters, a Stalin tank had sent phosphorus shells into a terrified mass of civilians huddled along the Angerstrasse.

I was exhausted. Sprawled on the ground, I had nothing left inside me, no wish ever to get up again. What for? Nothing made any sense. Nobody would come out of this cauldron alive; I was certain of that. It wasn't just that I was drained physically, I had also lost all hope and the will to live. I knew that I had reached the end of the road. It was over. Lying on top of corpses and in between them, it felt as if I was floating. I felt light and so close to death that, strangely, it appeared to be a welcome refuge. I had my eyes closed and looked inwards, fully conscious that soon death would gather me into his arms.

I am not sure how long it was that I lay there, it may have been seconds, minutes or even longer perhaps, but at some point the dreadful detonations all around tore me out of my numbness and into the ear-deafening reality of the slaughter, furiously ripping into the town with a ferocity not seen before. But, hey, what was that? Listen up! There . . . All of a sudden we heard a sound, a ringing pitched higher than anything we had become accustomed to during this battle. What was that? It was hardly believable but that sound, that combination of honking and tooting harked back to older times, to a different world. Was I awake? Was I in a dream? It couldn't be true, I kept telling myself, and yet, drawn to find out about these curious sounds, I lifted my head cautiously, tentatively, from where it had been wedged in between two corpses.

No! There was no doubt about it. I'm sure now, that that sound, that particular howling is not an illusion – it's real and it's a signal. Well, wouldn't you know it! The vibrations rouse me from my stupor. I prick my ears up: these are the notes of a well-known melody, I realise, which is meant for me. I'm not dreaming, it's coming closer, it literally goes through me and I recognise it as a trumpet fanfare calling on me to gather myself up and onto my feet. I turn around and I cannot, truly cannot believe my eyes. Storming towards me, swathed in a glow of fire, some supernatural being comes raging across the sea of corpses, swinging his sword right up to the barrier. No – it's not a dream

The evening situation report sent by radio from Ninth Army to Army Group Vistula on 25 April 1945.

A Ninth Army message explaining the intended break-out route.

and it isn't a ghost. It's a lieutenant! A young German lieutenant – an archangel circled by a halo of light.

Leaping to my feet while someone thrusts a carbine into my fist I scramble over the corpses and tear after the lieutenant. Hurrah! What has come over me, I wonder, but not giving it further thought I focus on what lies ahead of me. I must heed the obvious call to duty! Against all odds, I have to fight for survival – that's my mantra. All fear has vanished, making room for certainty:

> 'And if you challenge not this life,
> Never shall life be worth living.'   (*Schiller*)

And with this rallying cry resonating in my ears, I watch as men all around me, in front of and behind me, wounded men and those given up for dead, rise from beneath heaps of decaying corpses and gather in great numbers to form a spearhead. Brandishing our weapons and pressing hard on the heels of the lieutenant, we storm forwards as if possessed. Nothing, we believe, absolutely nothing can deter us and no shell nor bullet will hit us. Passionately screaming a bellowing 'Hurrah' we thrust towards the anti-tank barrier, cross over in great leaps and force our way to the other side, then disappear into the forest. This is how I survived Halbe, so help me God.

We're expected

Rottenführer Eberhard Baumgard

Late that evening the security company of the 32nd SS Volunteer Grenadier Division '30th January' was ordered to prepare for break-out. That's the unit I was attached to. When, towards the end of January, the Soviets had reached the Oder and indeed had crossed it at certain points, I had volunteered for the division despite my serious injuries; my condition had been disregarded and I had been declared fit for limited service. At the time, it was a matter of course to follow the motto drilled into us as German soldiers throughout the years. Always serve as if all of Germany and everything German depends on you and your actions. This is your responsibility . . .

Moonlight filters through the trees revealing sandy tracks as we are ordered to maintain our spacing while still keeping in close contact with one another. That's easier said than done what with us being enveloped by darkness except for a tiny bit of moonlight piercing through the cloud cover. How can we look out for the next man when we have to jump into cover at practically every step of the way? We cross a wide road. By now, the forest is teeming with soldiers who, it seems, have been ordered to stay put. Ahead of us Soviet artillery fire detonates. We are nearing the explosions while the explosions also seem to be moving ever closer to us.

The firing is vicious and relentless. Shells of all calibres detonate high up in the trees. They bring down tree trunks, whirl mounds of vegetation into the air and tear craters in the ground. Splinters whistle through the branches and flashes of gunfire light up the woodland. Fountains of earth spring up as shells explode and lumps of bark and wood hail down. The entire forested area is hit by a systematic barrage of fire. Ducking and leaping across the terrain pitted with shell holes, I stumble over a tree stump a split second before another explosion blasts through the woods. My progress alternates between diving into still smouldering craters and sheltering behind trunks.

Only one thought preoccupies my mind: I've got to escape. I mustn't lose close contact with the others. In the bright flashes of the explosions, I see silhouettes flitting about. There are only a few of them. Numbed by the ear-deafening shelling, I'm also paralysed by the fear of not connecting up with the lads. Could it be that I'm completely on my own? What of it! Push on! It would be a total joke if I were alone. Surely, I'll be able to link up with my comrades once I reach the front. So, banish all these negative thoughts and get on with it! Take cover, act on your instincts, run risks, find the next foxhole, leap into it, crouch down as low as possible and don't offer yourself up as a target for the explosions overhead. Be prepared, tense your muscles, sharpen your senses and get ready for the next jump, and then the next one. Don't waste time on reflection, don't even consider weighing up possibilities, and above all – have no fear. What matters is that you're filled with blind rage and, yes, this rage and an obsessive determination will get you through this, get you closer to . . . paying them back.

The disorderly flight of thousands of heavily loaded civilian carts mixed in with the retreating soldiers made any sort of organised resistance virtually impossible.

Above & opposite: Ninth Army's situation report to Army Group Vistula
of 26 April 1945

I make good progress ... until I suddenly trip and land in
a one-metre-deep trench. Dazed at first, I then come to and
much to my relief make out in the glow of the surrounding fires
motionless, waiting soldiers to the right and left of me. Weirdly,
I feel quite secure in this slit trench and all the more so because

the barrage of fire seems to be dying down. I note only a few explosions close to my hideout spot which tells me that Ivan is switching his artillery fire to a different section at the front. What do I care . . .

I haven't quite got my bearings, but can tell that this slit trench which had served a purpose until now will not turn out to be the ideal place for me in the long run. The actual frontline is quite a bit further ahead, so I set off. A few metres further on I come across a young Army infantryman kneeling close to the edge of a pit, helmet and face pressed against the muddy ground. Taken aback at this unusual sight, I thump him on the shoulder which makes him startle. I look into eyes full of terror. 'The first round is all done and dusted,' I try to reassure him. He gradually takes me in, realises that I am not an Ivan but belong to the SS. He forces a grin at me, then untenses, his face slowly relaxing with relief. He is obviously much heartened by bumping into another German who seems to be unperturbed by what is happening, and above all who's still alive.

'What d'you mean the first round?' His voice trembles. 'Oh, why worry,' I mumble and crouch down next to him. 'But yes, soon, there'll be the next one.'

'What? Are we trapped?'

'Most definitely, if we stick around here!'

He looks at me quizzically, clueless.

'If there's a way out, then it's at the front, at the front where they're shooting, d'you get it?'

I have straightened myself up trying to figure out the route along the trench. 'Let's move guys, we've got to push on,' I call out to the those lying there, but there's no sign of life from that direction. At that moment the firing starts up again. Ducking low, I pass by the motionless bodies on my left, who appear to be literally petrified. 'Get going, you lumps!' There's no reaction, no looking up, no looking at me. I don't see any injured men, only men who have been paralysed in spirit and body. Finally, I see a face staring at me. . . I'm hopeful but then look more closely at his expression – blank. I try moving to my right. Eventually, I've sort of had enough. 'Get your asses up, you lot! D'you want to push on towards the Elbe or d'you want to be sat here and croak?' Nothing, no response, nobody stirring . . . 'Fine by me,' I grumble, 'they'll shit all over you jerks if you don't watch out!'

I haven't clapped my eyes on a single one from my own troop. Have they advanced further? They must've done, I think, and climb out of the trench, calling out to anybody who'll hear. The young comrade follows me while I tell him what to do when under artillery fire. I say he's to do as I do.

Unhindered, we put a good distance behind us until we note a commotion in the wood. There are shouted orders but they sound more like prayers than instructions. Swearing at the lousy bunch of cowards before me, their collapsing discipline and their lack of fighting morale, I decide to press on and give the guy in tow one last chance. 'If you want to come along, I'll give you cover. If you want to stay put, you'll end up rotting away like the rest of them. You decide.' He nodded, obviously happy to trust me.

Though the firing was increasing, I felt heartened by having a comrade at my side. We Landser know the proverb: 'A German never likes to go it alone,' and recalling this slogan puts me right back into battle mode, into the thick of the attacks I lived through on the Ukrainian steppes. The moment a shell is fired I know whether it will hit the ground close by or whistle past above my head. I follow the path illuminated by the firing. Blazing fires, bangs of exploding ammunition and clouds of smoke and dust seem to be rising up from one location only. There, ahead of me, lies the centre of the cauldron. And my sixth sense tells me that that is precisely where the slaughter is unfolding, that it is there that our men are attempting the break-through, unless they've already succeeded in their mission. So, what am I waiting for?

Forwards, Grenadiers, Forwards!

Hauptsturmführer Paul Krauss

On a forest track, just short of the railway embankment at Halbe, I ordered the remainder of my unit's supply section, which had come to a standstill, to blow up the trucks in the rear. 'Distribute what's left over from the supplies!'

It was actually impossible to advance any further on our vehicles. But if we wanted to break out to the west, the only option was to cut through Halbe. A rumour spread that Wenck's army was situated somewhere near Zeesen and that we had to reach the main line of resistance. No matter what, we had no other option than to push into Halbe, most of which was already

The road junction in the village of Kehrigk. A Ninth Army airstrip was
not far from here during the retreat.

occupied by the Soviets. Together with another officer I intended
to conduct a reconnaissance of what our best route might be. After
ordering the leader of the supply company and his men to follow
us precisely twenty minutes after our departure, we set off and
reached some woodland just short of the Halbe station, finding
the area chock-a-block with German soldiers and civilians.

There, in front of us, along the railway embankment, stood a
red-brick building occupied by the Soviets who were busy firing
at our copse with machine guns and artillery. Swiftly scanning
the area, I found out what I needed to know. Most of our soldiers
were no longer carrying arms. They lay down or stood around in
groups, stunned, helpless or having decided not to do anything

to counter the barrage. I was not best pleased. I ordered the other officer to go back and rush our troop along as I was convinced there was a real possibility of breaking through there and then. I surely didn't want to lose momentum. The Russians on the other side and along the embankment didn't appear to be a significant threat . . . yet. I gathered around me a few sergeants, soldiers and civilians: 'I'll take over now. We're attacking in half an hour – that's our break-through!' (In circumstances such as these, half an hour seems like an eternity – but I needed to wait for my men to arrive as, without them the likelihood of success was small.) I then told those crowding around me that anyone prepared to fight, civilians included, should get ready. 'Whoever's still got a weapon and ammunition should shoot the living daylights out of this position. The rest shout "Hurrah!" My command: "Forwards, grenadiers!"'

Needless to say, my officer never returned with my men from where I had left them, but instead, I could distinctly hear a battle erupting from the woods. The agreed half-hour came and went and I simply couldn't afford to wait any longer, so I decided to break through with the comrades at my side. 'Forwards, grenadiers, forwards!' I screamed and charged ahead. And wouldn't you know it: the whole lot of them, soldiers, civilians, women and children started racing after me towards the Russians. These must have been so taken aback that they hardly fired in our direction, fleeing by the hundreds. We stormed forwards some few hundred metres past the station building and barely fired a shot. Then, suddenly, we realised that we'd made it – we had broken through. We had actually managed to cross the embankment without suffering any serious casualties.

We reached the forest for a second time. Elated by our recent success we dashed on but then came upon a sunken track, some two metres deep and 250 to 300 metres long: it was filled with corpses lying everywhere and on top of each other, German soldiers and civilians. Press on! That was the motto. But even here in the woods on the other side of Halbe, we saw mounds of bodies, some wounded, some dying. The entire area was being shelled by artillery, and rockets and mortars caused heavy losses. With Russian bombers and ground-attack aircraft striking from above, our lot disappeared into the thick of the forest. Either on his own or in small groups, whichever way suited him best, each and every one wanted but one thing: to head west, nothing but west.

Cohesion had nearly completely collapsed. All discipline had fallen by the wayside. I, to my credit, had brought out German

The site of the improvised landing strip near the village of Kehrigk.

men, women and children across the Russian battle line. That's at least what I kept telling myself. Not that there were large numbers of them, but I still felt satisfied with the break-through success I had achieved. My other hope was that the men from the supply troop might have been able to break through at a different location.

Now we were beyond Halbe a fresh rumour was spreading, that the Americans had reached the Elbe. All able-bodied men were to push forwards to the Elbe . . . and then fight both the Russians and the Yanks. What folly! Pipe dreams! But it was precisely those which motivated masses of people to stream towards the Elbe.

The Railway Crossing at Halbe

Rottenführer Eberhard Baumgart

We pass dead, wounded and despondent Landser. Cowering low, they seem like frightened rabbits, their eyes nervously twitching. Others stare down at the ground. Where have those men, those true Germans disappeared? Those fighters? To me, these jerks were nothing but wimps – worse still, assholes. They're just waiting for others to storm ahead, break out and clear the way for them! Disgusting!

With my comrade in tow and just short of the town, I reach a road leading past a timber yard. Meanwhile artillery fire continues above us, but luckily it's just harassing fire. I do note increased mortar shelling, however. Well, I could have done without that. Ducking low we hasten towards the crossing trying to be mindful not to trip over corpses. Sometimes we quickly jump over them, just like in an obstacle course, a grim analogy.

The closer we approach the railwaymen's hut on the left, the denser are the heaps of dead bodies. Good God, it must have been hailing down here! I've rarely seen such stacks of corpses in such a small area during all my war years . . . and then only in Russia. But there are no Russians around here, only Germans. It's a real mess.

I seem to be magically attracted to that little railwaymen's hut which lies to the left of the red and white crossing barriers sticking up into the sky. Could this be true? Are my eyes playing a trick on me? There in front of me, men were pressed tightly together along its length like a swarm of bees on a post. How many are there? Forty? Fifty? Have they gone totally mad?! 'They must be off their rockers!' I shout across to my comrade who has now caught up next to me. 'I'll take a closer look!' What from afar looked like frozen grains of salt turns out to be something indeed alive but devoid of any sense, literally . . . these wimps were in my mind nothing but empty vessels covered in grey uniforms. 'Is there any point in you scum of the earth?' I scream at them. 'D'you think you've really found a safe place? Safe from enemy fire?' There isn't the slightest reaction. What the hell? The flickering light of the burning freight shed illuminates the scene in a ghostly fashion. 'Guys, you'll bite the dust for sure, if you stay here. D'you want to go like sheep to the slaughter? Hasn't it sunk in that there's only one chance left: fight and break out!'

They don't comprehend what is being said to them. Some stare at me with a mixture of panic and confusion, their faces lined in dread, others turn on their side in eerily slow motion. 'Guys, why don't you understand? If we stick together, we're strong!' Nothing. The shelling intensifies and I make up my mind: if I want to avoid being a target, I have to get out of here. Anyway, as the saying goes: 'Whoever doesn't want already has. And whoever won't listen must feel it!' This cowardly bunch makes me want to

The forestry office at Hammer. This was the site of the Ninth Army command post in the later stages of the battle. The final orders from the HQ were issued from here.

puke. Turning to my comrade I spur him on. 'Let them suffer!' We push on.

There are only a few metres to the red and white crossing barriers pointing to the flaming sky like warning signs. The crossing is covered by what looks like a patchwork quilt, made up of corpses, grey-green uniformed corpses. Looking closer I only recognise German soldiers. Goodness, a bloodbath must have taken place here. My buddy, always at my heels, is quivering with fear. 'Onward, comrade,' I try to encourage him, 'Off we go through the middle!' Easier said than done as the dead are literally lying in the middle of the crossing and how can I blithely tread all over them? I have to get away from there, get my bearings. Wherever I look, right or left, I can see nothing but corpses, corpses in front of me at the crossing, to the right and to the left of me, over the tracks and in the track beds – corpses as far as my eyes can see in the darkness. And anyone stopping, yes, there's no doubt about that, he'll soon lie alongside them, that much I'm convinced of. It's also clear to me that Ivan must have purposely targeted this crossing as it's the obvious entry point to the town. The hits seem to have been precise, worryingly precise. 'Nothing to see here, comrade!' I say, dragging my mate along. 'We're out of here!'

I manage to tread carefully, placing my boots in between the corpses, but the closer I approach the crossing, the more difficult it becomes to avoid those who possibly are only wounded and waiting for help. I alternate between shoving the corpses to the side, dodging and tiptoeing as I can't be sure that all of these people are actually dead. The thought that I could squash a dying man nearly makes me vomit. Gritting my teeth, I shuffle onward, gradually picking up pace by swiftly treading over them as best I can. Not being able to make out exactly where I'm putting my boots down, I still try to avoid trampling on any upturned face. It's not that easy to find your balance while slithering around on soft and wobbly bodies. Reaching out my hand to hold on to my comrade, I try and steady myself so as not to slide and slip off. 'Man, oh man! What did they do?' I exhale, sighing. They must've been running to their death like lambs to the slaughter.

With every step we can hear squeaking, crunching and cracking. No matter how cautiously I move through this grotesque human web, I keep on hearing it: the squeaking, the crunching and the cracking. Damn! I swallow hard. How far does this morgue carpet reach? I feel nauseous. Damn, and damn again . . . but we'll soon have made it!

Briefly glancing to my right, I can see the storage barn next to the station building burning bright and, in the blaze, I can read 'Halbe' on the station sign. I'll never forget that name.

I can't get away fast enough. Hastily we follow a street and where it forks off, I decide to go left. After a few hundred metres, passing a church on the right-hand side, we've already put the town behind us. The road then opens into a pine wood, still aglow with raging fires and pitted by shelling that continues sporadically in the dark. I'm not bothered by it, though, as not much could be worse than Halbe, I figure. Also, judging by the hammering coming from various directions, the frontline is still a bit further ahead of us. And, in my book, where the shooting is taking place, that's where we need to go. Surely I'll come across some comrades from my section and there's nothing I want more than that.

Direct Hit

Rottenführer Eberhard Baumgart

I got hit at the anti-tank barrier on the way to Teurow. My comrade and I approached that particular barrier as we had seen two German tanks stationed there. Stuck and unable to roll to either the left or the right on this very narrow section of the road, they had just escaped the hell hole of Lindenstrasse. Turning back was not an option and, having lost radio contact to headquarters, they were left high and dry without further instructions. We two grenadiers wanted to hop on and take cover as the entire forest was teeming with Soviet infantry blocking off the break-out sector. At night and in such circumstances tank crews fear being without infantry support and exposed to the enemy.

A wrecked SdKfz 7 artillery tractor, capable of towing a heavy gun and carrying its crew, burnt out and amid a field of debris after a Soviet bombardment.

My worry is not the danger of being targeted in close combat. As expected, this anti-tank barrier halfway between Halbe and Teurow has long been the target of Soviet fire. Let's just hope the crews of these Panthers make up their minds. Once aboard the tanks we wait for things to start. Before too long they will, we think, and indeed they do: suddenly bitter fighting breaks out. Murderous anti-tank, artillery and mortar fire. Everything at once: whistling, blinding whiteness, explosions, pressure, smoke billowing through the night and ripping my legs off my body. Whirled around I am aware that what was once my comrade has now dissolved in that same whistling, blinding whiteness and explosion above me and which, pelting down, has lifted me off the ground and hurled me onto the tarred road.

I feel calm: I've been hit. No question about it. I can now rule out the uncertainty of whether or not I will survive this slaughter. Back then, posted on radio watch close to the Oder, I wondered about my destiny, mused about what the future might hold for me – on that day a call interrupted my daydreaming. Now I know, I know that I've been crushed, that I can depart this world at any moment. I feel no fear, I don't cry or cringe. Indeed, the relentless shelling barely enters my consciousness.

I've removed myself from reality and a different reality has taken hold of me, as I see my mother before me, I see her clearly as she's sitting at the top on the stone ledge beside the stairs going up to our front door. She sits there as if waiting for me. She's sitting outside, so that she can see me when I return home, turning into Kantorstrasse. The sun is shining on mother, it's a Sunday. She smiles at me and I feel elated seeing her like this. She is wearing her Sunday best. Gradually, the image fades away. I float. From above, I spot the home I grew up in, the cherry tree in the front garden, slightly forward of it the high wooden fence, all swathed in a bright and peaceful glow. Oh, how I wish to sink into this light, submerge, become one with it. Instead, the scalding sparks of a fire burn my crusty eyelids.

I try and open them, but am barely able to. Hot flames surround me, blazing fires, shelling, and the screams of medical orderlies. I actually feel let down by the fact that I'm still among the living. The pity of it all! With every heartbeat my numbness thaws. Once again, I'm aware of emotions stirring and memories of the most horrendous experiences come flooding back. With great pain I manage to lift my lids. Glued together with blood, they feel leaden. My lips have burst open, my mouth is bleeding, full of splinters, my teeth crunch on sand. I try to move my tongue so I can spit out the dirt, but I fail. I can't imagine what my face looks like . . . I don't want to. With my hands I tap my body and my fingers glide along the blood smeared on the uniform, it feels wet and warm, sticky – filth mixed with blood and sweat. I'm able to raise my head a little; sitting up is impossible. There's no way I can get myself onto my elbows and knees, Waves of pain rush through me. I don't even dare roll onto my stomach. Blood congeals on my thighs and feet.

I'm lying stretched out across the roadway, barely a metre away from the left track of a Tiger. I catch the crew exchanging comments on the devastating impact of the attack. I'm sure there aren't as many medical orderlies in the entire Army as are now needed here on the ground. What would a medic do for me anyway? Where in fact is my mate? He must be somewhere here, close by. Frantically I grope my way towards the tank. I hear shouts: 'Start up! Now!' Engines begin rumbling; the first tentative rattling of motors fills the air. Petrol fumes puff out of the rear exhaust pipes sticking out above me – enough for the engine to catch. I scream. 'D'you want to mash me up, you assholes!' The engine starts up and tongues of flame jet upward above me. The tank will reverse at the next moment when the engine is sufficiently revved up to get this humongous Tiger moving. Its left track will crush my rib cage and stomach – if I remain lying there. But then something jolts me into action. No, under no circumstances! Not this! I'm not done yet, I'm not finished. This mustn't be my end. It may not happen.

'You assholes up there, if you won't have me on the engine deck, then just for Pete's sake drag me into the trench!' There are some more guys jumping onto the back of the Tiger. They ignore me. 'You swines!' I'm alive, I don't want to be turned into mush – and certainly not by tanks. The monster looming above me vibrates with its metal armour shaking and all I've got left are a few seconds. I'm furious. But this propels me to shove myself to the side, clear of the tank tracks. I actually manage better

Soviet infantry being urged to the attack by a junior officer in heavily wooded terrain.

than anticipated, gliding like a snail along its path. Sliding while turning my head some 180 degrees, I manage to edge myself to a lying position, head first, towards the roadside ditch. Thanks to the camber in the road and leaning my body downwards while pushing with my hands, I avoid, at the last second, being run over and crushed. I want to press on and leave the road behind me. But once off, it becomes much more difficult to make progress and I'm not sure why. Groping around I realise that I no longer have the advantage of a slippy surface. What surface? Oh, my God! Horrified, I register what it was that has saved me! The path is smeared with blood, intestines, faeces and urine, with lungs, liver and muscles of comrades crushed flat by a direct hit. My lord, comrade! This is the second time you've saved my life! Your body took the full force of the direct hit, just a metre away from our position, and what has remained from you enabled me to slide along into safety and to escape being rolled over by our own tank. You are my saviour by default! I owe you my life, comrade, and for that I'll forever be grateful to you. Once again, I feel alive, albeit reduced to a stump.

With great difficulty I claw myself out of the ditch and then up the sandy embankment desperate to get an idea of what is happening. The tanks have roared off. I hear some moaning, see bodies sprawled out or coiled up and now have a clear view of the damned trap – the road barrier. There are still some soldiers roaming around on both sides of the causeway. I hear them being assembled and ordered to march. Then, all of a sudden it all starts up again. Looks like there's not a soul on earth who could give a damn about us.

I long for my lost rifle. Slowly, painfully, I lift my head. My unit is nowhere to be seen. There is so much flickering light around that I would surely spot them – but there's no trace of them. I don't think that I can take much more. I fumble around for my pistol, and thankfully my good old pistol is still on me. I draw it out of the holster to load it fully. Better safe than sorry, is what I go by. It wouldn't surprise me one bit if Ivan were suddenly to make an appearance. Carefully I tuck it between the second top and third buttonhole of my Army tunic. It' s not the first time I've considered making an end of it. But, before that, should someone attack me, I'll kill him first, that's my full intention.

Instead of Ivans I come across medical orderlies who flit from one wounded man to the next trying to provide whatever first aid they have available. Something akin to happiness flows through me. Looks like we're not completely on our own then, I think to myself with some relief . . . we haven't been abandoned after all. I call out to the medic and he waves back. 'I'll be with you in a moment!' He then approaches me, he's an Obergefreiter, and carefully turns me on my back. 'Let's see what can be done here.' I tell him that somewhere in my coat pocket he should find some bandages. 'Don't worry, mate, I'll put on a triangular bandage, that should do it,' and with that he shoves it underneath my back. Fingering along the lower part of my body I can feel that whatever is left of me down below is shredded to bits, burnt and wet – covered in blood. 'Get your hands off, mate!' he warns while tying the knots of the bandage and tucking it into my belt.

'Good luck, comrade, can't do much more for you right now, but keep your ears peeled!'

I wonder out loud whether I'll get away from here. 'Just don't give up hope, comrade!' advised the officer, trying to be encouraging, and with that he's gone. I can still feel his hand pressing on my shoulder while he's already attending to the next wretched guy groaning away on the embankment. It is at that moment that I realise that not all of the good comrades had been left behind at Stalingrad.

Only Those Who Forsake Themselves Are Forsaken

Rottenführer Eberhard Baumgart

I let my hand glide up and down my body and can feel that nothing has remained intact: not my head, my torso nor my limbs. I have been hit everywhere. The left half of my face in particular feels like rough sandpaper. Blood, grit and tar are glued together biting into my face like a smelly clay mask which prevents my eyes seeing through. Painfully I rub them clear to see nothing but a frightful scene.

Once in a while motorised rear personnel arrive from the direction of the barrier, just to reverse and tear away with engines howling and wheels screeching. As if hounded by furies they seem terrorised by the sight of soldiers lying stretched out to the right and left of the embankment like human wrecks. The night is brightly illuminated so it is easy for me to observe that those uninjured are at great pains to not look at us wounded, indeed, they ignore us completely. Swines that they are!

The whimpering, the groaning and the moaning cries for help die out without a single soul taking any notice. Nothing but the roaring of engines engulfs me. Cowards, the lot of them, pigs! Not one guy from the SS appears – damn them all! If I don't want to croak in this god-forsaken shithole then I've got to pull my socks up and get moving. Grit your teeth, I say. If you're half a man, then don't let yourself down. I roll onto my stomach, crawl to the edge of the road right up to the wet bit I know from before: 'The next asshole won't slip through the net!' I swear to myself.

With my left arm crooked underneath my chin, I lie in wait. Before long a VW Kübelwagen rumbles towards me and, slowly lifting my head, I watch as this god-sent vehicle stops right alongside me. The passengers, all Army officers, ignore me, however. Dumbfounded, as if struck by lightning, they stare at the road barrier.

Heated discussions ensue amongst the crew, all of them poring over a map on which they shine a pocket light. Fully occupied with themselves and their problem of wanting to connect with the break-through advance guard, they obviously want just one thing: to save themselves.

Slithering like a snail over the grimy path made up of corpses and blood, I watch the driver above me scanning the area. What must be in his view are, apart from the road barrier, the right- and left-hand slopes of the embankment plastered with the wounded and the dead. He doesn't see me. I, however, can well make out his look of total disgust and his impatience to get the hell out of here.

I have to make haste . . . without being noticed, I get close to the vehicle and, with my left arm, grab hold somewhere between the driver and the back seat. Grimly, painfully I pull myself up and with my last bit of energy I haul my body up onto my knees.

'Make room! You're taking me with you!' I yell. They glare at me with revulsion. Stunned, they stare at the ravaged 'me' who's escaped hell.

'I'm coming with you!' I bark into their faces without avoiding their eyes. Within a split-second I realise that these gentlemen

The forest road between Hammer and Halbe, seen in a modern photograph. Although much of the growth in the image is clearly postwar the scene is likely little changed from that before the battle started.

Former Unteroffizier Norbert Plewa's attempt to escape to the west came to an end at this point. He was taken prisoner with a group of comrades, but obviously managed to survive the rigours of Soviet captivity.

are out to save their own skins and don't give a jot about a low-down turd like myself. This, in fact, spurs me on.

Garnering all my strength I push my head to the height of the seat and then hoist myself up by wedging my right arm between the vehicle and my coat.

'Off, away with you – there's no room here!'

'Man, what are you on about!'

'Off!'

Someone slaps my wounded face and tries to push me away.

I've now got a good hold with my left arm inside the car and I'm determined not to let go – not for anything. Not over my dead body! I feel entirely within my rights as it is dishonourable for a German soldier to abandon the injured, it is, in fact, the greatest sin and contrary to the spirit of the motto 'My Honour is Loyalty'.

You bunch of miserable clowns with your pathetic red stripes – I'll give you what for. And fearing what might come next, I'm reaching with my right blood-smeared arm which had before so offended the officer, for my pistol. Right in front of his foul mouth I release the safety catch and just as he opens it wide I yell 'Drive on, or else!' The word 'reverse' got stuck in his throat. 'Just you dare!' I rasp.

Horrible seconds tick by – plenty for me to do my thing. I pull myself right up and clamber inside while not taking my eyes off any one of the four. There's no fooling around with the likes of me –which seems finally to get through to that despicable lot. Yes, fellows, it's eye for an eye, and tooth for a tooth!

They are paralysed by fear. The officers break out in a cold sweat while the driver seems to get it in one. All the better as far as I'm concerned.

Dragging, shoving and with immense difficulty I draw myself up. Strangely, the blood-smeared uniform seems to come in handy.

'Watch out, you bastards, if I hear even the slightest peep out of your dirty gobs, I'll kill the lot of you! All four.'

He must be a madman. A lunatic who's escaped from hell – that's what I read in their wide-open eyes. Pale moonlight and flickering fire illuminate the scene in ghostly fashion.

But I'm not a ghost. It's me, all right, a me who's determined to take anything on, to dare them all. At their slightest move, I'll pull the trigger.

In the meantime, I'm kneeling on the footboard. 'Make room!' I hear uncomfortable hemming. At long last they seem to grasp that they'll go to hell if that's what they continue to be – pigheaded .

The two officers on the back seats have already budged to the side, albeit unwillingly and disgusted – but I have the space I need to keep my elbow propped up..

'We . . . we can't squeeze up anymore.'

'Why can't you understand that?'

'Impossible!'

'Sure, it's possible!' I hiss and push the muzzle of my pistol into the neck of the front occupant.

'What you really should be doing, man, is helping me! That's what you should be doing!'

'But, but . . . don't you see . . . you're getting the seat all dirty, and my uniform!'

My face, contorted to a sneering grin, shuts them up a while and, without any support from anybody, I get myself into the empty space begrudgingly cleared for me. And wouldn't you know it: there's even a gap left between me and the genteel officers.

'Well, finally,' I scoff. I've triumphed.

Wedging whatever is left of my legs underneath the front seat, I try to balance and not slide down or fall out. It's painful to sit, but at least I do sit and, on top of that, I'm in a vehicle that's moving and that's what counts here at the anti-tank barrier short of Teurow.

'Off, start the engine!'

I rest my right elbow in my hip, allowing me to hold my Luger just at head height pointing at my neighbour. I've made up my mind: as long as I'm sitting here in this car, I'll be ready to shoot and whoever even thinks of reaching for his weapon, I'll shoot dead then and there. And finally it seems that the penny has dropped: they know that I've got nothing, nothing at all to lose while they've got everything, everything to lose. And they behave accordingly.

Ninth Army situation report sent to Army Group Vistula on 27 April.

The officer on my side is at pains not to come too close to me, not to smudge his precious uniform. Filthy asshole!

I won't bat an eyelid if I have to kill them all off in one go . . .

Well, their miserable fastidiousness serves me well – I now have plenty of room on the back seat of the VW Kübel.

The Army Medic at the Tank Barrier at Teurow

Rottenführer Eberhard Baumgart

What was it that took place during that fateful night of 28/29 April 1945 at the anti-tank tank barrier half-way towards Teurow? While defeated and decimated sections of all the service branches were pushed out of Halbe's Lindenstrasse, desperately seeking an exit point but physically trapped due to the narrow route, a further concentrated artillery bombardment threatened to wipe them out completely. Those intent on breaking through were quite literally going from the frying pan into the fire.

Tanks roaring up from the rear rolled unrelentingly along the roads squashing everything in their path, including anyone not able to scramble to safety, away from the killer treads of the steel tracks. That was also the night when desperate cries for a field medic briefly filled the air in the odd pause of the battle, and when the cries didn't go unheard.

Dazed by all the confusion and fear, those still ambulatory were possessed by only one thought: to get going and flee. Perhaps the panicked cries for help from the wounded and dying were nothing more than a reflex action, but, miraculously, they received a response: in the midst of this hell on earth, the appearance of an Army medic seemed like a god-send. In this ghostly hour after midnight, it turned out, not all soldiers lost their sense of humanity.

This, then, is the story of an officer who braved the inferno and who didn't waver upon seeing one of the most horrific scenes of this war, the town of Halbe lit up by the flashes of enemy guns and the flames of burning houses, collapsing ruins and smouldering shrubbery. It is the story of a man offering heroic support to so many of those lying there wounded or dying, the story of a hazy figure hastily flitting from one heap of human misery to the next, from road to ditch, from pine tree to mud path, offering words of

The forester's house at Halbe, about a hundred metres from the Halbe station and the railway crossing there that became the focus of so much ferocious fighting.

The signal box and rail crossing at Halbe as restored in recent times but the site of frightful scenes of slaughter in April 1945.

comfort and a warm pat on the shoulder signalling to the soldier stretched out on the ground that he was not forgotten and that someone was there to care for him. And then he rushed to the next and the next one. The wailing didn't stop.

I myself felt the touch of his hand. He was one of those human beings who had risen above his own self, who had responded to the call of duty and knew what it meant to be a German Army medic; someone who hadn't succumbed to the motto 'save your own skin'. Out of the dark, there he was, kneeling beside me rummaging in my coat for my triangular bandage then gently turning me on my side to knot the cloth firmly across my stomach before rolling me over again. 'I'm afraid I can't do more than that, comrade. I wish you luck!' And with that he was off again, tending to another injured man. That was the Army medic to whom I owe my gratitude.

'Are you the legendary Army medic from Halbe?' I asked a man forty-seven years after the Halbe slaughter entered our history books. Shrugging his shoulders, he claimed no longer to remember. His name was Herbert Gossmann, a local of Halbe.

While reports seem to suggest that only one Army medic attended those in need after the horror had ended, helping thousands of wounded and dying, surely there were more?

By the self-same token, nobody recalls seeing even one Army priest who performed his Christian duty – and there were a number of them in our armed forces. Where were they during those nights?

'I'd Rather Die than be Taken Prisoner'

Martin Kleint, very young infantry soldier of the 'Kurmark' Division

25 April 1945 – beyond Halbe. Though we had found cover in the night in the hollows of the forest we had to assume that the Russians were on our tail. It was also possible that they had dug themselves in west of Halbe. In any event, we didn't know where to turn. Exhausted, we simply stumbled on with only one goal in mind: to get away from the burning inferno, to flee this doomed town.

Soon we had reached the Lübben–Königswusterhausen Autobahn, crossing it with utmost caution. It was towards midnight. Once safely on the other side, we threw ourselves to the ground and went to sleep while others stood guard. As dawn broke, we woke the sleepers up with a boot to the ribs and slowly, with the sun briefly breaking through the clouds, we got our bearings, figuring out which way was west.

We reached the edge of a wood where we came across some freshly dug foxholes, quite obviously abandoned just a few hours earlier, one of them even had a full mess kit and a pot of jam in it. At the far side of the wood stood a small house [probably the Massow forest warden's lodge] where a white flag was raised. This was the first white flag we had seen. This seemingly idyllic scene was abruptly disturbed when the door of the building was torn open and some twenty Russians stormed out to seek cover in the nearby wood. Flinging the mess kit including the jamjar to the side, I threw myself to the ground, positioned my MG and fired at them at a range of about 100 to 150 metres.

Before most of us could even grasp what exactly was happening, the enemy had all but disappeared with only one man left behind prostrate on the ground, the top of his scalp razed off by an MG burst. When I came closer, he was still groaning. Overall, quite a dreadful sight to behold. But I was only vaguely aware of it as something else left us totally stunned and shattered to the core.

About one hundred metres away from the Russian, who meanwhile had expired, lay a naked and raped girl, hit in the head by a bullet. A soldier in German uniform was hanging from a pine tree next to her. None of us could utter even so much as a word. Dumbfounded we stared at the two dead people, at the raped girl and the hanging soldier who looked at us with glazed eyes. We cut down the dead man and slowly set off, but had made up our minds that it was better to die than to be taken prisoner.

~~Geheim~~ 349

Geheime Kommandosache

Fernschreibname Laufende Nr.	536 / 0250	
Angenommen Aufgenommen	Befördert:	
Datum: 19	Datum: 19	L.d.W./EO.
um: Uhr	um: Uhr *wenden*	Datum: 24.April 1945
von:	an:	Nr. 0994/0620
durch:	durch:	
	Rolle:	

Bermerke: KR-BLItz

Fernschreiben Posttelegramm von
Fern/pruch

Abgangstag	Abgangszeit		An	1) Heeresgruppe Mitte 4) Heeresgruppe Kurland 2) Heeresgruppe Süd 5) A.O.K. Ostpreußen 3) O.B. Südost 6) A.O.K. 9

Bermerke für Beförderung (vom Aufgeber auszufüllen) | Bestimmungsort 7.) Pz. AOK 3 8.) Korpsgruppe Reiman

An alle Heeresgruppen des Ostens.

Chef Gen.St.d H Nr. 25o1/45 g.Kdos.

Verbrecherische Gerüchte aus dem feindlichen Lager behaupten
Waffenstillstand mit Amerika und ähnliche, den Kampfwillen lähmende
Dinge. Mit aller Schärfe ist gegen diese Gerüchte und ihre Verbrei-
tung einzuschreiten. Der Kampf geht bis zur siegreichen Entscheidung
weiter. Der Führer steht an der Spitze der Entscheidungsschlacht
um die Reichshauptstadt und damit um das Schicksal des Reichs.
Er vertraut auf Kampfgeist und Entschlossenheit des deutschen Heeres
Wir werden dieses Vertrauen nicht enttäuschen.
Dieser Funkspruch ist mit allen Mitteln unverzüglich an alle Dienst
stellen weiterzugeben. Der Chef des Gen.St.d.H. i.V.gez.Krebs.Gen

Obkdo der Heeresgruppe Weichsel
Ia/Nr. 6057 /45 geh.Kdos.v.24.4.45
F.d.R.
gez. Eismann

Nicht gr In: F.d.R.
Hauptmann bei Aufnebers | Fernsprech-Anschluß bei Aufnebers

As late as 24 April orders were being issued anticipating victory on the
Eastern Front and telling soldiers not to believe rumours to the contrary.

117

Many Civilians Commit Suicide

Major Brand, 21st Armoured Reconnaissance Battalion,
2nd Panzer Division

Some 2,000 leaderless officers and soldiers and probably as many civilians of all ages, men and women, linked up with this battalion. We made a renewed break-out attempt on 29 April early in the morning, with several initial successes near Halbe. The Russians finally retreated having suffered heavy losses. At the Autobahn crossing west of Halbe our entire unit fell into a Russian trap during the night. There were hundreds of dead and many half-mad civilians; the situation was horrific. We had three fatally injured in my own command tank. Control was lost, morale disintegrating, units badly disorientated. Women were being raped to death by Russians in the forests and on the roads.

'Seydlitz Troops' made a further appearance. Seydlitz men would eavesdrop on orders, mislead their own units and inform Russian troops of our positions. Leutnant Bühlman dropped dead right next to me; Leinhard and Hoffmann had been killed just shortly before. Generalleutnant Marks was injured. He had ordered Reuche to blow up his half-track and dismount. Our men didn't have any cover and were heavily shelled; most perished on the spot and the rest were taken prisoners. Rueske's legs were blown clean off; what's left of him ended up alongside the road. Leutnant Frese was shot in the stomach. Those last two were both given morphine. I suspect they were taken prisoner.

Many civilians committed suicide. I myself was seriously injured and while I was treated with morphine compresses, Wartermann took the lead.

30 April – the remainder of what was once our unit disappeared in the swamp. We left the injured in the care of an

Army medic who was intending to bring them back west. At 0300 we marched off with Leutnant Melzer, Stach and five men – all injured. We were taken prisoner in a surprise attack during the night by Mongolian troops. They moved us to some Russian tank position. What followed was an example of how Russians have fun. We were stood up against a the wall along with some SS officers; the SS officers were shot. Melzer and I were spared but then had an entire day of cross-examination by the Soviet secret police.

'Comrades, Surrender! For You the War is Over'

Alfred Blombach, Battlegroup 'Schill', 1st Battalion,
86th SS Volunteer Grenadier Regiment

On 28 April I was injured during the break-through in the cauldron of Halbe.

Late that afternoon we reported, ready for our advance. Just before Halbe we were attacked hit by heavy MG fire from our right flank. Russian tracer bullets were biting into us. I remember thinking that I'd never survive this. But, in fact, there wasn't an alternative and, with no time even to think, we launched our attack!

The Russians entrenched in town seemed not to have expected us. It was obvious that we'd taken them by surprise as we came across a field kitchen with its pots still steaming in the courtyard of one of the farmsteads: obviously we'd stopped Ivan enjoying his lunch. It almost looked like they prepared it to welcome us! We didn't have time to taste any of the Russian food. Thanks to the sudden appearance of three tanks to take the lead we kept going through Halbe.

The anti-tank barrier blocking the western exit from Halbe was only
a few metres away from this bakery in April–May 1945

I have to admit that the tanks, I seem to remember that they
were Tigers, filled us with renewed courage. We managed to
keep the road out of Halbe to the Autobahn open. But at what
cost! Russian troops were concentrated in the forests to the right
and left and had unbroken observation of the whole route to the
Autobahn – they brought down a massive barrage from an entire
artillery brigade. The fearful slaughter of Halbe continued.

On top of that, we came under continuous attack by Russian
infantry assault teams. Flames shot into the air and rifle fire
whipped through the trees. The blazing scene was filled with
the horrible cries of the wounded and the din of exploding
ammunition. We had a difficult time defending ourselves. The
calls of 'Assault guns! Forwards!' still ring in my ear. 'Get yourself
into the firing line!'

That was probably the last thing I heard before I was hit. I was aware of a strange gong-like sound and then blacked out. I'm not sure how long I lay there unconscious. A mortar splinter had pierced the back of my steel helmet (that must explain the gong). Shrapnel had also penetrated my lower right arm and my back. It looked like I owed my life to the steel helmet and my haversack!

Once I came to, I realised that I was lying next to dead comrades in a ditch beside the road. But who had bandaged my head? Who had dragged me off the street? Some unknown Army medic must have taken pity, and I will forever be grateful to him, as I would surely otherwise have been run over by passing vehicles.

The crew of a VW Kübel driving by heard my shouts, and stopped and took me aboard. Continuing on at a snail's pace we were repeatedly exposed to Russian attacks with our infantry, squeezed into a stationary column. forced to fight them in close combat. By then dawn had broken and Russian aircraft now pinned us down as the bitter fight unfolded.

I was shifted to a *Sankra* [ambulance], but after a while it too came to a dead stop due to the roadway having been torn apart by a bomb. Trying to circumvent the crater, the driver looked for a way through the trees, using a path meant for transporting logs, but before long his vehicle got stuck in the Märkisch marshland and before we knew it the driver had disappeared without as much as looking back. Of my group, all injured and now abandoned, only three were still ambulatory: two guys from the Army and myself. Hoping for the best, we set out.

Reaching a clearing, we were stopped in our tracks by shouts of 'Comrades! Surrender!' and with that two Russians plus a guy from the Nationalkomittee Freies Deutschland emerged from a copse some hundred metres away.

My two Army comrades approached the Russians but I didn't feel like it and stayed put. It took me only a moment to realise

Soviet infantry desperately seek cover from German fire during a woodland battle.

my predicament, though: if I crossed over, the Russians would probably shoot me at point-blank range, but if I tried to escape, they'd definitely try to shoot me in the back. One way or another, I'd likely be shot dead. So in the end I also walked up to the Russians.

I no longer felt any fear, or rather, I had no time even to think about it. Meanwhile the guy from the NKFD had vanished and it turned out that the Russians were keener on my wristwatch than on my pistol. Members of an artillery company took us prisoner but, other than having to hand over our valuables, we remained unharmed. We were moved to an assembly area in the forest and ordered to join the many German soldiers already held prisoner there, but despite craning my neck in all directions I couldn't spot a single man from among my erstwhile troop. These were all Army Landser who were probably the same ones who'd tried to help us back there with their bellowing Hurrah! It had all gone wrong: they had apparently run out of ammunition, thrown away their weapons as a result, and thus weren't able to shoot, or so they told us.

While I was still looking around, three Russian soldiers approached me, separated me from the rest of the prisoners and indicated that I should follow them. Ha, I thought to myself, I just hope they shoot straight. But it wasn't so simple. First a Soviet officer interrogated me, though there was little I could tell him and no longer having my paybook on me didn't help me one way or the other (we had all burnt our paybooks before embarking on our break-through assault).

Then they ordered me to follow three Russians. Resigned to whatever would befall me, I trotted behind them, eventually arriving at a farmstead. Many injured Russians were lying in the courtyard which apparently had been turned into a dressing station. Told to wait in a shed, I realised that no one had actually noticed me, and because of the coat I was wearing I wasn't immediately identifiable as an SS soldier.

My turn did, in fact, come when a Russian soldier ordered me to follow him. In a room now converted into a surgical ward, I had to take my coat off which made me quite anxious as I feared they'd soon figure out who I was: underneath the coat I was fully kitted out for war. Fortunately, no guards seemed to be around and much to my relief I was dealt with properly and

An SU-85 tank destroyer during the Battle of Berlin.

professionally instead of having to suffer through the dreaded 'special treatment'. I was stretched out on a table and given ether as an anaesthetic but it didn't seem to make me any less aware at first of the Russian lying next to me who screamed incessantly. When I came to, though, I was sitting on the same seat as before in the shed, fully clothed, bandaged and cleaned up. An Army medic informed me with gestures that a sharp-edged splinter had been removed from my head and the Russian doctors had done a good job.

The next morning a column with hundreds of prisoners of war was marched off. Luckily I didn't have to walk and was allowed to take a seat next to the driver of a horse and cart. For good order an MG had been placed on the rear of the vehicle – of which there were several, all distributed along the marching column, which was also flanked on both sides by Russian soldiers ready to shoot.

The Russian comrade placed next to me on the bench didn't stop talking but I didn't understand a word he was saying. From his friendly expressions I gathered that he was trying to reassure me: for the likes of me, he intimated, the war was now over and I could return home. This was the same message called out to us by the crews of the *Stalinorgel* driving in the opposite direction – on their way to Berlin.

What about us? Suddenly this amiable guard of mine gave me his pocket knife, pointed to my collar patch and the eagle on my sleeve and motioned me to detach them. It'd be better . . . Of course, he was right. It so happened that when we arrived at the next town Soviet soldiers – men and women, especially the fierce *Flintenweiber** – picked out those from the column of prisoners who were wearing the black uniform with the 'death's-head' emblem. These were mostly comrades belonging to the tank units.

Such checks and selections continued to take place all the way to Luckau but I never found out what actually happened to those who were dragged away. Once we reached Luckau, the column was divided up: I ended up in a POW hospital, once a school building, where we were taken to the large gym and told to lie on the floor. Russian guards handed us some bread and soup, but otherwise left us to it. During the night, though, when they were drunk they would come and look for women and as there were some female communication auxiliaries and Red Cross nurses with our lot. We lent them our coats, trying to make them unrecognisable as women. Some, sadly, didn't escape and I'll never forget the screams of those unfortunate girls. There was no way for us to help them.

---

* Usually translated as 'shotgun women': female Soviet soldiers.

The Russians celebrated the end of the war with a lot of booze, though all we prisoners received to mark the day was a thin noodle soup. On 8 May those of us who were ambulatory were assembled for transport to the prisoner-of-war hospital Sagan-Stadt. Our guards were armed Polish police who didn't wear a uniform but could be recognised by their red and white armbands. Compared to those bastards the Russians turned out to have been absolute angels. We marched for hours each day and were driven into empty buildings for the night. There was no food whatsoever. This went on for many days. Farms and the houses in the villages were deserted. Every now and then we chanced on something edible, often raw potatoes, and once we even got hold of a thin cow which we went ahead and slaughtered. Having been granted a longer stay-over, we could finally eat our fill, though the Poles grabbed the bulk of meat for themselves.

Some comrades managed to escape. I don't know whether they were successful in the end. Comrades who couldn't keep up the pace, and those who fell by the wayside, brought low by their injuries or just sheer weakness, were probably shot dead by the Poles. In any case we never saw them again, but would always hear shots fired behind our backs.

I still owned a pair of boots so walking was not a problem for me. But this too was not to last. Near Cottbus, during a brief stop, Russian soldiers turned up and set about frisking us from head to toe. Though there was not much for them to take, it turned out that my boots caught the roving eye of a Red Army soldier . . . Surprisingly, the guy was so friendly that he actually swiftly replaced them with a pair of shoes – I'm not sure where he got them from. They turned out to be much too big and from then on marching became torturous.

Prior to being dumped so to speak in Sagan, there a stopover that lasted unusually long. They counted us and counted us again and I'm not sure how many had gone missing. But once we were handed over to the Russians, somehow the number of prisoners was the same as at our departure. Probably the Poles randomly picked up men and women from the mobs and refugees wandering around on the side of the road to replace the shot escapees – it was that simple.

Targeted in the Break-through Battle

Rottenführer Eberhard Baumgart

Reversing, we rolled back down the road to Halbe. The embankments on both sides of this fateful dead-end were covered by tall grass but gradually flattened out. The road was pocked with craters, large and small, forcing our vehicle to zigzag between them. Out of the corner of my eye I took in what was going on outside, but was more focused on the passengers sitting in front of me 'against their will'. Stony-faced, they stared ahead. Being threatened by some random Obergefreiter with a pistol and now being treated as hostages had all come as a shock to them, I realised, and had completely disorientated the poor sods as they had only ever been used to blind obedience.

It seemed to me they didn't actually know quite who they were dealing with. My uniform – now bare of the collar patch and the eagle both on the sleeve and above the breast pocket – might have actually irritated them. Had they spotted my belt buckle? I wished they knew who they had before them: a Rottenführer from the *Leibstandarte Adolf Hitler**– oh well! They'd find out

---

* Established as Hitler's bodyguard detachment, by 1945 the *Leibstandarte* was the senior Waffen-SS Panzer division, an elite combat unit, but one also responsible for numerous horrific war crimes and atrocities.

127

A Red Army anti-tank and light artillery unit on the advance. The towing vehicles are mainly American-supplied Dodge and Willys types.

anyway that there would be no fooling around with the likes of me and quickly learn that I considered them traitors and cowards and that if they so much as dare to think about dumping me back in that hellhole at Halbe, I'd take them down with me.

At the edge of the blazing town we turned left into a forest path. Streaming in from all directions as if through a funnel were entire units, various smaller groups of soldiers, horse carriages, trucks, self-propelled guns, towing vehicles and armoured reconnaissance half-tracks. We got wedged in among all that and kept having to dodge past fallen trees, broken trunks, branches and treetops blocking the road. After a while I could make out an empty field on my right. Our attempt to advance along this forest aisle teeming with soldiers and civilians was getting more difficult and more exasperating with every metre we put behind us. Rumbling over craters and fending off dispirited and unruly troops was increasingly unnerving. Finally we came to a complete halt about a hundred metres further along with tree trunks lying right across the path making it impossible to continue.

The officer at the front leapt out. More as a reflex than a response to danger, I shoved my pistol into the ribcage of my neighbour finding an easy spot to put the barrel just above his Iron Cross first Class. Meanwhile my 'comrade officer' had returned from reconnoitring the area in the darkness lit only occasionally by flames flickering across treetops. 'Everyone! Dismount! If we're to get across these tree trunks, we'll have to do it on foot!'

Turning to me specifically, he motioned me to get out too. 'You've got to help as well, you know!' 'Frankly,' I retorted, 'I couldn't give a shit about helping you on your way. As for me, I'm staying put and that goes for my neighbour here as well,' I said, prodding him with the pistol. 'You'll forgive me if I . . .' mumbled the officer sitting on my far right and I nodded in reply. He jumped off. All I could gather is that he was a very high-ranking animal. I mean really high up. The two men now outside the vehicle shouted to some Landser to come and lend a hand to lift the vehicle, engine still running, across the obstacle. A little at a time we managed not more than a few miserable metres and ended up not achieving much more than blocking anyone who came afterwards.

Meanwhile I became increasingly aware that somewhere behind us, a reconnaissance vehicle, possibly an eight-wheeler, was coming closer. I was familiar with the sound one of those made and knew how powerful they were. Where we had failed it would surely succeed. If only we were part of that crew! The bigwig officer ordered the driver to keep to the right of our VW – and it turned out I was correct: it was indeed one of those eight-wheeled armoured cars I knew from the reconnaissance unit. The commander stood up in the hatch, saluted, and pointed behind the turret where there were Landser lying packed back-to-back below the tank's frame radio aerial: all injured or worse, I assumed. There was no room on the 'deck of the injured', barked the commander. My officer now well and truly came into his own once more, issuing stern orders which resulted in a several infantrymen emerging from the dark. They were told to put me on the eight-wheeler and I certainly had no objection – on the contrary. But, rather be safe than sorry, I thought, and kept my pistol at the ready until I had been heaved up and across, floating for a moment in the air. Only then did I tuck away my Luger to squeeze myself in a bit better.

Men made space for me, swearing and reluctantly moving themselves over ever so slightly to the side. As I unavoidably bumped into bodies on my right and left, I heard moans and groans everywhere and the heavily wounded cried out in pain at every move. 'Dreadfully sorry, comrades!' I could barely fit myself in between some mangled bodies. I fumbled for my leather pistol holster just to make sure, but actually felt relatively safe up there. My wounded hand was throbbing and burning – the skin of my forefinger had been torn loose and was hanging down limply, so I tugged it off. The armoured car started rolling, the rear deck where I was lying vibrating from the heavy roaring of the engine. Much like a caterpillar it got its wheels over one tree trunk after another and then, gradually picking up pace, it headed into an empty meadow. From there the driver was able to accelerate rapidly. We were now heading into the heart of the battle. Could I hope for more?

Shells howled around and exploded in front of, next to and behind me. Then we made a zigzag dash. Splinters pierced the armoured skirt, branches were hurled to the ground, whole trees fell. The artillery fire sent shards of red-hot shrapnel and burning phosphorus flying around us. Lying there helpless like strips of

The armoured car Baumgart remembered riding on in the retreat would have been a similar design to this SdKfz 234/2 model but may have been equipped with a different gun and turret arrangement.

pastry dough, we kept our heads tucked in like turtles, arms stretched out by our sides, fingers tightened to a fist. We were face down on the steel, all our senses on high alert.

Bullets from machine guns and rifles joined the shellfire blasting all around us. This was the start of the break-through: the enemy fire somehow intensified and shells of all calibres burst through the air, while beneath me the engine howled. The driver pulled out all the stops – the commander screamed for him to advance and he screamed back 'Understood!' while giving the engine full throttle.

Still numbed by the deafening explosions, I suddenly felt myself grabbed at the shoulders, pushed to the side of the vehicle and then held there. I was totally confused by the fists violently

The crossroads in Halbe. Whether on the Teupitz or the Teurow direction the escape route always led over corpses.

pummelling me but then I realised that I'd been brutally shoved to the edge of an armoured car which was being pelted by Russian artillery fire. And before I know it, I've pretty much turned into a bullet trap.

'Pigs! Despicable, cowardly pigs! You say you're wounded? You're a bunch of shitheads!'

'Shut your gob – you're a goner as it is!'

'Not yet!'

In the meantime, I've drawn my pistol. When confronting the enemy, all I had needed was luck, I thought to myself, but dealing with the 'comrade' before me was quite a different matter. I had to be on my guard.

'Shit,' I thought, 'I better realise where I am. This is not my team. These are idiots! If only they'd at least use me properly

– if they'd act like proper panzergrenadiers – but just showing cowardly behaviour – that's pathetic.'

I registered the fact that the sounds of battle were fading. There were some sporadic bursts of enemy fire, but gradually stillness descended. The driver slowed down and I dared to lift my head. We'd made it! We'd broken through!

As it was cautiously manoeuvred down a steep embankment, the armoured car came to a stop, practically upside down. I tried to balance myself, managed to grip some bars, but with one jolt the vehicle bounced across a ditch and ended up in a near upright position. We crossed what I thought was a wide road, then I saw it was an Autobahn, and scaled the embankment on the opposite side.

By now barely able to keep my eyes open, I reasted my chin and right cheek on my right arm which wasn't as badly wounded as the left one. Throughout the night we kept rolling west. The wheels were rumbling, the engine was humming, and though there were oil and exhaust fumes all around me, I felt content.

Lying Wounded in the Forest for Days

SS-Oberkanonier Hans Schaller

If you ask me, it was on the evening of 28 April that our army became a leaderless horde. It was at that point that every single unit leader was left to his own devices to decide for himself how he would get his men out of the growing chaos. For me, that meant the end of 506th Nebelwerfer Battalion.

An Oberscharführer from the 'Nordland' Division had linked up with us, intending to attempt the break-through alongside us. Though our rocket launchers had been blown up and abandoned we still had one vehicle left with fuel in the tank and that's how we were able to reach the assembly area at Halbe. That was, in fact, a fortunate move, as total mayhem reigned everywhere else. Landser roamed around like herds of sheep and not a single one of them had the energy left to fight. The motto was: I won't harm you . . . if you won't harm me. This was a mistaken, fatal line of thinking as we'd soon find out.

At some point during the 28th we arrived at a forest path short of Halbe – the assembly area designated for the break-through planned that night. We had only one aim: to reach the Elbe so as not to be taken prisoner of war by the Russians. There were simply too many horror stories doing the rounds which filled us not just with fear but cold terror.

One of the forest roads leading to the Autobahn to the west of Halbe.

It was a calm afternoon. Famished and assuming we would reach the Elbe the following day, we gobbled down our iron rations. Rumour had it that all break-through attempts made over the previous days had been successful. An Army Oberst joined us at around 1600 hours, introducing himself as an officer who knew the plan and had been nominated to lead the break-out attempt. He ordered those of us who were on foot to follow behind the tanks for the break-through. Being artillerymen, we had no experience of infantry fighting, but we were certainly prepared to do our bit if properly led. However, not having any weapons other than our old Kar. 98 rifles and their bayonets we were rather useless. We had no automatic weapons, no hand grenades. We did, mind you, have the willpower to make it through to survive.

By the time we lined up behind the tanks we had already discarded most of our belongings – no longer needed . . . we had even left our haversacks in our vehicles. There we stood, determined to meet this last challenge with nothing to our names except our rifles, bread bags and two filled waterbottles each.

Then, at around 1800 hours, it all kicked off. The Russians pounded the middle of the assembly area with a heavy barrage. The tank crews disappeared into their hulls, closing the hatches. The Russians blasted the area relentlessly with their heavy 15-cm guns until, in the trees right above me, a shell exploded with devastating effect – two dead and four heavily injured men. I was lucky, however. When the shooting began, infantry Landser who were set to follow the tanks showed me how to take cover and thus actually protected me, as otherwise I would have been killed right then and there.

I didn't really feel the hit, though I did notice something pressing into my thigh and a warm trickle running down my leg. It was only later, when I tried to disentangle myself from the older Landser half-lying on top of me, that I realised the extent of the injury; the other guy, with his guts hanging out, must have received the full impact of the blast. Twice he called for his mother, then it was all over – that's how quickly one dies! (This image has remained in my memory throughout my life since then.)

It was impossible for me to get back on my feet . . . I just didn't know what was the matter, seeing as I had no experience with this. Surely, I must have broken some bones, I thought. 'That's it then . . .' Someone pulled me out from amongst the dead and wanted to get me to a field hospital set up in some ravine, but I refused. As it turned out (I only heard this from eyewitnesses I met in 1991 at a reunion of the division which was operating in that area at the time) this saved me a second time that day, as the Russians murdered all the occupants of the hospital – staff and patients – either shot or killed them with bayonets.

An Army medic arrived carrying with him a small package of bandages and dressings. As I was intent on being taken west, he had to find a way to put me on a truck – that wasn't so easy, as most of the vehicles still in working order were attached to the units to which the wounded soldiers belonged and they, of course, had priority over me, the odd one out. But the medic somehow prevailed. Just before lifting me up he quickly gave me an injection. The rest appeared to me as in a dream: the continued shooting, the explosions, the devastation. The truck moved forwards in repeated spurts of a few metres with the constant stopping and starting causing me to lose track of time. I was completely disorientated.

Dawn had broken when I came to. I can still remember the railway crossing at Halbe: the entire area was burning, dead bodies were strewn all over the place, many civilians among them, mostly refugees. Judging by what I observed these folks

The escape route towards the Autobahn heading for Teurow.

had got rid of all their belongings, probably realising that most of what they owned would become irrelevant in this break-through attempt. What counted was to save one's skin! Had the break-through failed?

Meanwhile, more injured were loaded on to the truck. We were on our way! Somewhere close to Halbe, however, in the middle of a forest the vehicle suddenly came to a stop. The driver disappeared and along with him the entire group of the 'gravely wounded'. It seemed that all of a sudden these guys were fully able to make their way west on their own.

Four of us who really were seriously injured were left behind. Nothing at all took place during 29 April. It must have been 1 May when a German civilian turned up, telling us that he'd been instructed to collect all the vehicles from the wood. He said

Soviet SU-152 self-propelled guns advancing. The mobility and firepower of these weapons made them very effective in close-quarter fighting.

that soldiers would soon arrive to retrieve the wounded. With that, I was placed on the ground but still didn't know the extent of my injury. All I could manage was to move backwards using my hands, as any other movement was immensely painful. I had sort of given up by then, but good fortune wouldn't allow that.

The Russians scoured the forest. These guys were, by the looks of it, an elite unit, all of them tall, strong men and they clearly knew what they were about. One of them approached me but was only interested in my valuables: my confirmation watch, pure gold – which, at the time, meant a great deal to me and was a precious memory – now changed ownership. The Russian spoke sufficient German to let me know that the 'SS bad people, comrades come and bumm, bumm, bumm!' It was only at that moment that I realised I was still wearing my SS collar patch. But, lo and behold, the Russian gathered some food tins and together with a fur-lined SS officer's coat flung these in my direction. Seeing that the nights were still chilly despite the wonderful spring weather that had set in, the coat came in quite handy and luckily, whilst recuperating in the field hospital, I was able to hold on to it. Later on, at the beginning of October, I managed to swap the coat for a pair of crutches which enabled me to escape to the west.

Among the tins the Russian had brought to me, there were two of asparagus – the ultimate luxury. Otherwise, generally, it wasn't hunger that plagued me, in fact I hardly ever felt it, but the thirst was torture. (Later on, I would always relish drinking the liquid from an asparagus tin. That is exactly what helped me quench my awful thirst at the time.)

Then it all came to pass as the Russian had predicted. Red Army soldiers from all kinds of ethnic communities, from the Soviet Union and Mongolia, started emerging and it was now their turn to trawl through the woods searching for valuables. They rummaged through the living and the dead. A badly injured man lying near me, for example, didn't want to part with his wedding ring. A shot put an end to that. My new boots found a new owner but I didn't need them anyway! It was a different story, however, for my officer's coat, which I skilfully managed to use as a pad for sitting on, and which no one took away from me.

Russian women also deserve a mention here. The Red Army deployed women too, even in battle. While we derisively called them *Flintenweiber*, they actually formed part of their regular troops. This was the first time the Soviet ladies were introduced to western flair and, while men focused on watches and the like, the women would pounce on nylon stockings which would flap ridiculously bunched up around their legs, as they, of course, had no clue how to put them on properly. Silken petticoats peeped out from underneath their uniforms and, to be honest, had the situation for us wounded guys lying prostrate on the ground not been so serious, we would have had a good laugh.

In the end, I was mighty lucky to survive. Those who were wounded but hadn't suffered serious injuries were gradually transported away until I was the last one left lying there. For two whole days I was completely on my own in that wood thinking this was the end of me. Finally, on 6 May, some passers-by, they were civilians, came to my rescue and brought me to a bathhouse. Another two wounded men had also been transferred there. Finally, after many days, I received some food and drink. The nights were disrupted by drunken Russians every so often barging into our shed and wielding their submachine-guns. 'Where woman? Where Missy?' We heard the screams of raped women, but couldn't help anyone.

On 8 May I arrived in Gross-Köris, a makeshift field hospital. That was the first time I received proper medical help, thanks to the local doctor. Up until that point it was only the bandage the medical orderly at Halbe had wrapped around my injury that tided me over . . . now surgery loomed. An upturned locker became the operating table and I watched as the doctor lifted my leg with one hand, and then, when he let it go, it limply flapped onto the table. I yelled the ceiling down, but we both knew what the score was: something had severed my thighbone. In fact, it was a piece of shrapnel measuring 5 cm long and 1 cm thick which he removed before sewing it all up. And after that he bandaged it properly.

Once again, I must admit to having been inordinately fortunate, despite the serious injury I had suffered. While I was hit by shrapnel in the thigh, it hadn't damaged any major arteries. Had it penetrated a centimetre further to the side, it would have been a different story and I would have died from blood loss within a short time. My parents would never have heard from me again and, like so many others, I would have ended up in a mass grave near Halbe – an unknown soldier.

Even to this day I feel sick when visiting the graves of fallen soldiers, as I know from personal experience that during the break-through at Halbe my life was hanging by a thread.

Thinking back: I lay seriously wounded in the forest for eight days; on the tenth day I finally received medical attention. This ordeal seemed to last an eternity and if you survive something like that, you know you're damn lucky.

My Suspicions Are Confirmed

Hauptsturmführer Horst Mathiebe,
32nd SS Volunteer Grenadier Division '30th January'

Today there's no doubt in my mind; it's a fact: once the higher echelons of the army saw how serious the situation was, they were only minded to save their own skins, regardless of what might happen to the troops under their command.

Perhaps I was guided by a guardian angel who made me do the right thing at the right time, as otherwise my battalion, as well as a huge number of other people, would have been taken prisoner by the Ivans. Along with my battalion, I was 'blessed' with the task of providing cover for our division on its retreat.

The last successful attack took place around the Streganz brickworks where a camp for French POW was situated. Suddenly the Ivans showed up. As we were, luckily, concentrated in battle formation, I ordered an immediate attack and we gave chase across the POW camp. Hans Kempin (then commander of the division) will remember this as, had the Ivans succeeded in breaking through, the division would have been stuck in the pocket without any escape route. In fact, at the time, Kempin radioed me with his compliments for this brave operation.

The escaping troops and civilians were spread across both sides of the Autobahn on their way from Halbe towards Teupitz.

Near Hermsdorf I was ordered to secure the retreat across the Dahme, close to the Klein-Hammer forest and this was the last order I was able to receive – then . . . radio silence no matter how hard the operator tried. While we didn't have to deal with the enemy during the night and there was no call on us to fight, we still felt abandoned. As dawn broke, fearing being overrun, I ordered my men to force their way towards the Klein-Hammer forest warden's lodge where we reached the bridge just in the nick of time. Seconds later it was blown up.

A good distance beyond the bridge we reached a fork in the road and I well remember hoping fervently that I had chosen the right path! It was the one which would lead us to Halbe. We survived relatively intact . . .

Herbert Gossmann, Army Medic from Halbe

Rottenführer Eberhard Baumgart

This man ended up being part of the medical team attached to the 'Grossdeutschland' Division trapped in the cauldron and involved in the break-through battle in and around Halbe. In the midst of this inferno, he was charged to remain with the medical team posted in Halbe and help those who were too weak to move, injured or defenceless. Yes, he stayed. Yes, as a German soldier he felt committed to follow orders, do his duty and obey far beyond the time when there were no longer any German orders being issued or to be obeyed, when the oath committing a soldier to serve and give allegiance to a leader had fallen by the wayside. He simply did his duty as a human being and as a comrade. He obeyed his conscience!

The Soviets recovered their wounded and were probably extremely preoccupied doing so. For fear of an epidemic, they ordered the surviving Halbe inhabitants to get the dead buried immediately. As far as the victors of this war were concerned, they turned their backs on all this, having deliberately decided to abandon German wounded in the roads and streets, in the gardens, houses, cellars, in the barns, the stables or in the woods – everywhere where they lay crippled or injured.

Some Halbe residents turned informer and chummed up with the Soviets – mind you, around thirty men from the town were detained and then imprisoned in NKVD camps. Others, considering themselves 'liberated', emerged from the Halbe ruins not knowing what the future would hold for them, among them women and girls who would be exposed to rape. Those were the men and women who would in the following days fulfil their moral duty.

In their midst stood Herbert Gossmann, soldier and Ober-gefreiter – surrounded by children, people of Halbe, refugees and old men and women who had escaped the slaughter. This soldier had chosen not to flee, nor did he swap his uniform for civilian clothing: he was a plain soldier with a Red Cross armband tied around his blood-stained grey-green Army jacket. After the still frightened Halbe inhabitants cautiously, tentatively crept out of their cellars and shelters once the eight-day slaughter had ended, he became a well-known figure. Suddenly, there he was, busy bandaging the wounded, distributing medication and giving tetanus injections.

This was not a man who stood idly by waiting to be called upon, nor was he somebody who wanted people to be desperately

A Red Army heavy artillery battery ready for action in the spring fighting in 1945.

beseeching him before coming to their aid; instead, he readily and freely offered his help and efficiently sought ways to reduce the crushing misery of the wounded who had been caught up in the cauldron. The mere fact that someone like him was living in their midst was heartening to these people who realised that someone was prepared to shoulder this herculean task. They were awed. The sense of belonging had, it seemed, survived the collapse, and some decent people still wanted to save whatever was left to save. His requests turned into orders, appealing to people's conscience and gradually, under his instructions, order was restored: the school, the church, restaurant dining rooms, larger cellars and any other building that still had an undamaged roof – all these were turned into temporary field hospitals and Red Cross stations to house the wounded brought in by the inhabitants, mostly women, who had gone out to pick up the bodies with carts or stretchers.

Gossmann went beyond personal patient care. He also organised children and old folks into teams to search for food, for medicines and bandages, blankets and clothing. Women and girls were allocated to the soup kitchens and one day, out of the blue, he came up with the idea of recruiting 'Red Cross auxiliaries' who'd take on all kinds of jobs and assist with the more than one thousand gravely injured patients.

It is hard to imagine: there were one thousand people lying there with injuries of all kinds, and there was only one medically trained professional in attendance: Gossmann. Day and night he looked after them, barely taking any food or drink, hardly ever changing out of his clothing. A thousand badly injured patients and only a single medic who knew how to dress their wounds, administer intravenous injections, and beyond that even dared – was forced to dare – to carry out operations to remove bullets and fragments.

Soviet artillerymen with a 76.2mm divisional field gun during street fighting near Berlin in 1945.

The women who lived through those times remember Herbert Gossmann to this day: our Army medic from Halbe who was inundated with demands to care for the wounded, who didn't stop ministering to the desperate through days and nights – these were the stories told long afterwards. 'The only thing he did was dress wounds, distribute medication and give injections. Between operations, we shoved some pieces of food into his mouth, a few sips to drink just so he wouldn't keel over, so he would continue toiling away – as what would we have done without him?'

After a while, the only ones left in Halbe were the most seriously wounded, as those who could walk or be moved had either made their own way to the Teupitz field hospital or been transported there as prisoners. There was a brief period when

Gossmann was supported by another qualified man, though he was a dentist, but he soon disappeared as well . . .

Often those who were collecting the wounded would chance upon injured Red Army soldiers whom they would then also take to the field hospital and place under Gossmann's care. Before too long, the local Red Army commandant officially recognised the Halbe emergency dressing station as a hospital and put it under his protection, but towards the end of July 1945 it was closed down. During these months Herbert Gossmann had become a citizen of Halbe and would remain living there after the war, working in a munitions clearing unit which, unsurprisingly, involved highly dangerous work.

Gossmann spent many years working in this risky profession when, one day, as he was trying to defuse a stick-type incendiary bomb, it exploded, reducing his right hand and arm to a charred stump. Well before his time, he thus became an invalid.

Forced to Step over Dead Soldiers

Erika Menze from Märkisch-Buchholz, aged seventeen in 1945

Sunday, 29 April. Everyone was just running around, moving and acting automatically, stunned and disorientated. Once in a while I'd think: please let me come out of this in one piece! Many injured soldiers were sitting or lying on vehicles driving past me. Just short of Halbe . . . we kept being pushed to the edge of the forest . . . we had to take cover repeatedly in shallow ditches. Mud and slush splashed around us . . . I vividly remember crossing the railway tracks (by Halbe Station) and what I saw was horrible. Tanks were rolling down the Lindenstrasse, the wounded were stacked up high and one of them tumbled onto the hard concrete

... then was crushed flat by the tank following behind, so that the next tank rolled through a pool of blood. There was nothing left of the soldier. This happened within seconds.

The pavement near the Drassdo bakery was covered in discarded equipment and corpses – all German soldiers. Along the house fronts many dead bodies, still clad in uniform, were stacked up high at an angle – I had to step over dead soldiers ... no cobblestone was left uncovered.

This was a horrific image ... towards lunchtime, all hell broke loose with splinters whistling through the air and shells exploding everywhere, above us, to the left of us and to the right ...

Menze survived the onslaught of the Soviets unscathed and managed to break out of the cauldron via Baruth the next day.

Hauled onto Kleinheisterkamp's Panzerspähwagen[*]

Otto Boomgard, SS Alarm Anti-aircraft Detachment, later with 550th Anti-aircraft Battalion, and then 32nd SS Division

By the time we'd taken up position near Halbe few of us were left from our second battery. We didn't have any of our original weapons either, with the last deployment of our 3.7-cm guns having been where the road forks off south of Königs-wusterhausen. What I want to say is that from then on each of us was pretty much left to his own devices. In any event, the way I managed to get through Halbe was by following two half-tracks, led by one of the big ones with a major in the commander's position.

---

[*] Panzerspähwagen = armoured reconnaissance vehicle.

A wounded Berliner and a female companion, whether a partner, friend or relative is unknown, seek refuge during the last stages of the battle for the German capital.

Building work on the postwar Autobahn between Potsdam and Beelitz. Some of the fleeing Ninth Army troops and civilians managed to link up with Twelfth Army near here.

We got through Halbe relatively unhurt, then made a dash for the wood, advancing swiftly despite a barrage of fire from all sides. During the night we were hit by a hail of shell and mortar fire. I got a splinter in the knee making it impossible for me to move, though until today I don't actually know exactly how it happened. But seeing as all this took place during a lull in the fighting, somebody actually noticed that I had been injured, stopped, shoved me up onto one of the armoured reconnaissance vehicles and then carried on. Once inside the hull I became aware how absolutely packed it was with injured men so I had no choice but to remain standing on one foot while holding on to keep myself steady.

After a while, I got chatting to an Unterscharführer – as it turned out the only one there who was willing to fight. He originated from Schleswig-Holstein. Intermittently we could hear shots being fired from an MG 42. Some time passed before it actually dawned on me that I had landed on Kleinheisterkamp's vehicle, and not only that, he had with him his entire family, his wife and two children, I seem to remember. Gosh, I thought to myself, will this end well? But there was not much for me to say and we made good progress during that night.

Suddenly we came under heavy anti-tank and machine-gun fire and within an instant the reconnaissance vehicle in front of us exploded with the turret being lifted off and hurled aside. All were dead. The Unterscharführer grabbed his MG and I got hold of a rifle and together we kept on firing. But then it was quiet and we continued rolling on across forest paths and country lanes just hoping for the best, really, as the driver had no clue where he was heading. Once we emerged out of the morning mist, there were no more Germans in front of nor behind us. We were totally on our own sitting on our half-track in an open expanse. What now?

Oh well! We didn't have long to think about our predicament as in such situations there's no set procedure to follow so we decided to give in to our desperate yearning for sleep: find a spot where we could lie down and just close our eyes and rest. Once we had reached a pinewood, we all descended, first Frau Kleinheisterkamp, the two children and the Unterscharführer and then me. Though I still felt the hellishly painful throbbing in my knee, I was fortunately able to put weight on my legs and hobble along.

<u>L a g e o r i e n t i e r u n g</u>   12.Armee

Die Zurücknahme eigener Truppen zwischen Mulde und Elbe
auf das Nordufer ist bis auf örtlichen Brückenkopf Koswig planmässig durchgeführt. Der Amerikaner fühlte über Gräfenhainichen
nach Norden bis Wörlitz vor.

Aus Wittenberg und nördlich davon angreifender Feind in
Grieben und Pilzig eingedrungen. Beiderseits Gross Marzehn angreifender Feind hat den Raum ostwärts Göritz erreicht. Im Raum
Niemeck starke Bereitstellungen. Der Druck auf unsere Front
westlich Treuenbrietzen hält an.

Der Feind im Angriff auf breiter Front im Abschnitt Kotzen
bis Linum mit Schwerpunkt bei Kotzen, das verloren ging, Pessin,
Königshorst und Linum.

Von Norden konnte Feind in Potsdam eindringen.

In Berlin setzte der Feind seine konzentrischen Angriffe
planmässig fort, Nördlich der Heerstrasse ging Charlotten-
burg verloren, Kämpfe am Halleschen Tor und Bel-Alliance Platz.

Eigener Angriff drang mit rechtem Flügel weiter nach Osten
vor, nahm Salzbronn und Elsholz. Um Beelitz harter Kampf. Nördlich davon stehen Spitzen der Div. Scharnhorst am Eisenbahnkreuz
6 km nördlich Beelitz. Angriffsspitzen der Div. Hutten haben
Ferch genommen. Eigener Stoss entlang des Schwielowsee noch in
der Nacht.

Verteiler:

O B
<u>Chef</u>
<u>Ia</u>
O 1   zugl.f.Ktb.

A Twelfth Army report notes that its troops can advance
no further to the east.

Walking a short distance into the thick plantation, we concealed ourselves behind a cluster of densely growing bushes some two to three metres high. I overheard the Obergruppen-führer say, turning to the Unterscharführer: 'Rather than be taken prisoner, I'll kill myself.' Drained, in pain and dog-tired, I flung myself to the ground and instantly fell into a deep slumber, as did the two or three comrades beside me.

Suddenly I was torn out of my sleep by Russian voices. It looked like Ivan and some of his comrades were on our tail. I leapt up, the Russian fired and I . . . no, I didn't keel over . . . I merely get a scratch, from a branch digging into my back, just above the shoulder blade. I was just lucky. What must have happened was that the Russian's bullet had been slowed or deflected by the tree and only a broken branch hit me. I had to act decisively and within a split second I was making a dash for it as best as I could – out of the plantation, zigzagging towards the forest with the Russian hot on my heels. *Stoi! Stoi!* ('Stop! Stop!') he yelled but he didn't shoot and I managed to get away.

That all happened around lunchtime, but don't bother asking me today where it all took place and on which day. Thinking back, I'd venture a guess: perhaps it was somewhere in the woods north of Baruth. Hastening out of the pinewood, I could still hear shots, but who the hell knew who was shooting at whom and when and where? All I remember was running for a few hundred metres before hiding underneath some brushwood. A little later on I made my way through the Russian lines in the dark.

The Russians Reach our House

Willi Haenecke, ex-mayor of Halbe

When I got to the top floor I watched through the window as an assault team, approaching from Klichs Teich, moved directly towards our house. I bounded down the cellar stairs shouting to all gathered there: 'They're coming!' The room went dead silent as we went through some anxious moments. We knew that all the Russians had to do was throw a hand grenade down the staircase on entering and we'd all be done for: fourteen people tightly packed next to each other. It would be a bloodbath.

We could hear them upstairs. Some guy said something in Russian which sounded like a question. Old Wagner responded in a language I didn't understand. Waving to us, he indicated we should go upstairs with him, so Paulus and I followed with our hands up. Nine men were standing at the top, aiming their sub-machine guns at us, with the leader addressing Wagner who seemed to be fluent in the language. Later on, I learned that Wagner originated from somewhere along the Polish border, so spoke Polish and, though Russian is different, he could converse with the intruders. They wanted to know whether there were any soldiers down in the cellar, Wagner translated and then assured them that the only people sheltering were women and children and they should, he said, check for themselves, but much to our surprise the men declined.

Paulus had some tobacco stuffed in a paper bag on him and asked Wagner whether he should offer some to the Russians. Once again, we were taken aback when the Russian leader shook his head and instead fumbled in his breast-pocket for a pack of cigarettes which he, in turn, offered to us. Nobody had quite expected that and we gratefully accepted. As the saying goes,

A shell dump near Halbe. Clearing abandoned artillery ammunition after the end of the war was an enormous and essential task, but also highly dangerous.

as long as one can have a smoke together, nobody will get shot. While all this translating was going on, I meanwhile scrutinised the squad's commander, whose face was dripping in sweat. They had come across the school courtyard, their weapons at the ready, keeping a look-out in all directions. Surely this hadn't been enough of an effort to make him sweat so much, or was it the tension and all the commotion? Was it something more sinister?

As far as we were concerned, all we felt was relief. When heading up the stairs, we'd feared for our lives and surely, had the Red Army men lost their nerve, we would have been dead meat. So who'd want to sit in judgement?

They cleared out and I was left with the feeling that they were well satisfied with the outcome of this encounter.

That same day we would receive several more such 'visits' from the Russians. Thanks to Wagner's linguistic abilities we'd

A cross marks the grave of a German officer and of
thirteen unidentified comrades. Nor is the date
(or dates) of their deaths known.

always be able to reassure them that their comrades had already
been by and so they'd move on.

After a while the troops disappeared altogether. From my
viewpoint, their behaviour had been impeccable throughout. But
there were other visitors seeking, among other things, women
and indeed finding them. Such nightly 'visits' left their mark,

though Ella hid behind the beds of the children and remained 'unscathed'. Wagner's niece hid in a cupboard on the second floor and also survived unharmed. As for the other women and girls – they had to obey and go upstairs.

'Hitler Kaput'

Hilde Neufert, Halbe, aged twenty-two in 1945

In the aftermath of the fighting around Märkisch-Buchholz the Russians ordered local men and women, boys and girls, to bury the dead, though bury would hardly be the right term to use.

In our yards we had a repair unit working on all kinds of vehicles the Russians had recovered in the woods and brought along for fixing. One day, a Wehrmacht ambulance arrived filled with corpses. We had to unload them and noticed that all, besides having suffered injuries, had been shot in the neck. Under the supervision of Russian guards, we were instructed to throw the dead bodies into bomb craters and pits and then cover them over.

There was a large bomb crater right next to our house. When it was full to the top, we gathered some Christmas decorations which an officer had found discarded in the house, balls and ribbons and such like, strewed them over the sand and trampled them down . . .

I remember as if it happened today:

One day we removed some soldiers' bodies from a small wood at the edge of the town and, to make transport easier, laid out the corpses in a row by the roadside. Suddenly a tank appeared, turned off from the middle of the street and rolled several times over the row of corpses – back and forth, several times, back and forth, practically flattening the bodies of the dead. As if that wasn't enough, the tank finally swivelled around on the remains, mashing them into the sand. The commander of the tank, an officer, leant out and yelled at us horrified bystanders: 'Hitler kaput! Wehrmacht kaput! Soldat kaput! Nix mehr da. Ha-ha-ha!'

Then we were ordered to pick up the remains of the bodies with our bare hands and drag them into a shell hole.

'I'll Try to Get Some Milk for the Children'

Willi Haenecke, ex-mayor of Halbe

The noise of the battle had been raging for several days and nights but now subsided. The gun mounted in the garden had fallen silent. Once, when I dared to climb upstairs, I scanned the area with my binoculars but could see nothing moving. The silence was rather frightening. I returned to the cellar and simply announced that I was hoping for another quiet day. 'Then I'll try to get some milk for the children.'

Despite the calm, this was a difficult decision for me seeing as nobody knew how the occupying forces would react to some civilian wandering around. Equipped with my milk jug I set off the following day towards our farm and, trying as best as possible to remain unnoticed, I chose not to walk along the street but to approach the farmstead from behind – via the Wursthof. From there, it was but a few metres to my home, should in fact something remain of it.

Crossing the sports ground, I saw the first of the dead. Krappe's villa had burnt down completely. A tank stood on what had been the railway tracks, next to it several corpses. All of them were SS men – and their faces had already turned dark brown. I walked along the path I used to take on my way to go fishing and noticed that the houses on the Wursthof were still intact. Then I turned into the street. What I beheld was so utterly dreadful, so unspeakably awful that my eyes welled up with tears – but far from being embarrassed I'd claim that tears were the only human reaction possible as the image before me could never adequately be put into words. A gruesome slaughter had taken place here and I could only hope that nothing like it would ever come to pass again. I still remembered the scene from just six days prior, when I left my farmstead and wasn't able to cross the street for all the troops crowded there. It seemed as if the area that was heaving then with the hunted and desperate masses was now shrouded in death and dust. The street seemed to have frozen in time, with the dead piled alongside the houses leaving not a single flagstone of the pavement visible. In the road lay vehicles of all kinds, equipment discarded in heaps, dead bloated horses, a Tiger tank shoved half-way up a lime tree, but there were also Red Army tanks. Squashed flat in the middle part of the street lay everything that hadn't been able to escape the tracks and wheels of the fleeing vehicles and then their pursuers, which had run over anything in their way. If I wanted to reach my farmstead I would be forced to tread over dead bodies – which I did.

Burying the Dead Around Halbe

Hans Jabschinsky, from Neudorf near Teupitz

As a sixteen-year-old I must have been pretty resilient, I'd say, because, thinking back, someone like me wouldn't have lasted otherwise . . . not through the collapse and all that resulted from it, neither physically nor emotionally. It wasn't as if we'd had never seen any action before; me and my mates, we'd experienced fighting first-hand – for example when I was an infantryman with the Volkssturm who were positioned at the access ramp to the Autobahn. None of the concepts of life and death, wanting to survive and being able to survive, clenching one's teeth – were alien to me.

I therefore didn't really mind much, nor did it bother me, when the Russians allocated me to a burial party. If the dead lay in a trench, we just covered them with some slabs of turf, if they were huddled in foxholes, we shoved some moss, bark or pine needles on top of the corpses as it all had to be done swiftly for fear of an epidemic and also because of the dreadful stench. One couldn't open any windows at the time.

So we dragged the dead and the amputated body parts – many women and children amongst them – and tipped them into pits, pushed them into makeshift graves, only minded to get rid of them as quickly as possible. Sometimes we came across a hollow where the dead lay criss-crossed on top of each other – and we simply covered them with sand before rushing off to clear away more corpses. We weren't meant to put up any markings on the sites – so at least we didn't waste any time with that stuff. Nothing was recorded either. What seemed important to the Russians was that none of us remove any identity discs or paybooks. That was strictly prohibited.

Salvaging the remains of the tank crews was a story by itself. If there was a particularly terrible smell coming out of knocked-out tanks or assault guns it signalled to us that the crew were still inside. But there was no way we could see anything for all the flies and swarms of carrion birds – once we opened a hatch, we'd find the inside literally teeming with those creatures. As soon as you lifted the lid, you were engulfed by a cloud of blowflies – the heat was sweltering during those May and June days in 1945. It was a nauseating task. We had to pull these poor sods out from

A German soldier lies in the smashed remains of his defensive position
with an unfired Panzerfaust at his side.

wherever we found them: crouched on seats and burnt down to coal, hanging down from ammunition racks; often we'd have to scrape off mangled body parts stuck to the inside of the armour. More often than not we actually couldn't really make them out, we'd only smell them … they stank to high heaven in those steel morgues of theirs. It wasn't a matter of just climbing in and fetching them – far from it. But as the proverb goes: necessity is the mother of invention.

Equipped with long-handled rakes with sharp steel tines that were used in the olden days by farmers to spread dung across the field, we set to work. But this of course was not farming … disentangling rigid bodies from the inside of a tank while blinded by flies was hideous work. It turned out, though, that the old soldier I was assisting had a way to get round this: he'd find a German hand-grenade – plenty of them were still strewn around – drop it through a hatch and with that the fly issue was resolved for the time being. We then set about hacking away with our rakes at the mass of mutilated, barely recognisable human bodies, slowly pulling them to the outside. Oh God! It felt like tearing at a mass of sticky bodies glued together; guts spilled out, corpses fell apart, a rib cage would tumble down. The job was relentless. Again and again, we thrust the rake into the clump of contorted human remains trying to clamp the tines to a body and then shove it out of the hatch while being overwhelmed by the putrid odour of decay.

Just you go ahead and try doing this for hours, days, for weeks on end while retaining your soul, while remaining an honest human being.

Burying those flattened by tanks was, comparatively speaking, child's play. They'd be the next ones we put into the ground. To put it bluntly, we were only able to recognise that a corpse was lying on the ground once we'd come across the pattern of a human body covered in flies – much like a silhouette. How is one to explain that?

What had happened was that the tracks of the advancing tanks rolled over what was once a human being, a soldier, squashed him into the dirt and after several weeks a shimmering and buzzing swarm of flies descended and covered the mushed body shape, *his* body shape: head, torso, arms and legs. Often, we'd find a flattened steel helmet and a mess kit crushed into the ground close by. We scraped this whole lot onto a tent-half and shoved it into some hole between the trees.

The dead horses were more difficult for us to deal with. It is just impossible to get the bloated corpse of a dead horse, legs sticking up, into the ground. Luckily there were all kinds of vehicles dotted around the area which we were able to get running. Attaching the carcasses to the rear, we pulled them to grass or sand pits and once we had dumped them inside with their legs still rigidly spread upward, we chopped these off. Everything needed to disappear down below as fast as possible.

The Halbe Mechanic

Eberhard Baumgart

Fifteen-year-old Heinz Jabschinski from Neudorf near Teupitz should, at his age, have been starting his apprenticeship in some craftsman's workshop. Instead, he was busy burying some of the corpses carpeting the fields of death around Halbe. And yet, throughout his life, he'd remain faithful to the battleground which was to define him.

Inextricably connected to the shot-up vehicles and the shattered weapons discarded in heaps by the Ninth Army and

A typical scene in the woods around Halbe and Märkisch Buchholz after the fighting finally came to an end.

strewn across paths, tracks and farmland, he remained in the area always.

After the victorious Russians hastily buried the bodies, they set about retrieving weapons, equipment, ammunition and vehicles and, for good measure, robbing the dead. It should be noted, however, that the defeated certainly didn't hold back either, albeit acting secretly, above all when it came to plundering food, tinned goods, clothing and appliances.

In these post-war months Heinz Jabschinski became an expert in engine repair and mechanical reconstruction, a master of his trade without ever having completed an official apprenticeship – nor did he ever receive a diploma or certificate. All he had under his belt was experience gained as a helper for the Russians in the aftermath of the Halbe break-through battle.

Dealing with abandoned goods wasn't something Jabschinski had intended to do as a career, but seeing as the Germans had to turn what the Soviets considered worthless into a commodity, this is precisely what Jabschinski did. Transforming broken rubbish into useful scrap he went into what was to become a lucrative market. However, he not only traded in old metal, but skilfully rebuilt what he had amassed such as trailers, Kubelwagen staff cars, and many other types of trucks and cars, tanks, tractors and motorbikes and he made good money selling them on. If he wasn't able to find a particular part that would fit the restored machine, he would simply manufacture a replacement piece basing himself as closely as possible on the original design.

At first, he provided reconstituted trucks fuelled by gas made by burning wood and then expanded to refurbish military vehicles equipped to transport lumber. A few of his models – motorbikes and reconnaissance vehicles – were later on used in war films (with himself often appearing as an extra) before being moved to the exhibition halls in the Dresden army museum.

The Moment I Stood in Front of my Farm

Willi Haenecke, ex-mayor of Halbe

It was only when I stood in front of my farmstead, that it all began to sink in. The fence had been knocked down and, standing there, I was surprised I could actually see the open fields. I was confused for a moment – I had never been able to look that way before – and then I realised why. There had always been a large barn there blocking the view.

It was at that moment that I fully understood what had happened: it wasn't just the one shed which had been razed to the ground, but two. The only structures still standing were the stables, usually home to my cattle and horses. Upon entering the first, all I could make out were dead cows. Then my eyes fell on two cows standing on their feet with – what a miracle – two baby calves – probably born during the battle.

But there was somebody else in the stable – in the corner of the middle corridor an older man had put up a camp bed. 'The owner must have fled,' he informed me matter-of-factly, 'so, it's down to me to give the animals some carrots and water, and anyway it's warmer in here.' I explained to him that I was the owner and that he was welcome to continue looking after the cows while I rustled up some food for him.

Our oldest horse, twenty-five years old and named Hans, was still alive and occupied a separate stall with a crated manger. His early life had been tough, but once with us, we'd only rarely used him for really heavy work and he still looked healthy with a plump figure and smooth skin. Two horses were dead, and a young one, a two-and-a-half-year-old stallion from Schleswig-Holstein, had gone missing along with his harness. I was certain that wherever he was his master was making him work, even though he hadn't been broken into hauling loads. It's only been a year and a half since I went to get him from Trebbin, I thought wistfully.

Then I went over to the remains of what had once been my pigsty. It was a simple structure with red-brick walls, the ceiling made of slats covered by heavy plaster mixed with some straw so that it stuck together. Above the sty we kept our bales of hay – mostly from the second-growth hay harvest. The ceiling had collapsed but the walls were still intact. Everything else had fallen victim to the flames – machinery, equipment, 1,500 kg of potatoes, a large number of hay and straw bales. But, lo and behold, a second miracle had happened: all the pigs were alive

A collection of anti-aircraft and other ammunition ready for disposal.

somehow, among them a sow with two piglets, though their bristles had been singed by the fire. Thanks to the heavy layer of plaster, the worst of the heat couldn't spread. When the ceiling caved in the fire must have been practically extinguished.

Another surprise awaited me on entering the main building of our estate. I opened the door to the lounge and there, in the middle of the room, stood a properly laid table: six plates with cutlery alongside, six wine and six liqueur glasses. An officer of the Red Army sat at the table, busy shaving himself and not in the least bit perturbed by my appearance. I was so taken aback that words actually failed me until I finally stuttered: 'Guten Tag.' Without so much as looking at me, or even responding, he continued to groom himself. This sort of encouraged me as I had expected to be booted away; feeling emboldened, I continued inspecting the house for anything broken. We owned a large mirror which hung between the two windows with a view down onto the courtyard and it was a treasured heirloom from my uncle Wilhelm. Indeed, it hadn't been touched and the top part of our buffet, almost entirely of glass, had also survived with only its door slightly askew.

Before we'd left our home so many days ago, we'd asked ourselves what a soldier would do if he came to our house and needed plates and cutlery? He'd open one of the glass doors, of course, and would help himself to what he required, we said. If the door is locked, however, he'll simply reach for his pistol and smash the vitrine. But if we leave it open, he won't have to do that, and so we left the key in the lock. Paper was strewn all over the floor and some broken records as well – but none of that was important to me.

Before leaving, I threw a glance into the bedroom and here too the dressing table with its three-part mirror had remained intact. The bed frame, however, was burnt at the edges. Only later did we hear that a fire had started in the bedroom and that old master tailor Wedel and pensioner Voigt had doused the fire with a few buckets of water.

Without being noticed, I then left my home.

Noodle Soup for the Victors

Report of a Halbe citizen, recorded by Eberhard Baumgart

It'd only been a few days since the battles in the streets had died down; the invaders, now our occupiers, hadn't yet left and it seemed that for better or worse we had survived. That's when some Red Army men who had set up camp in one of the farmsteads still standing requested a celebratory soup dish be cooked for them, a noodle soup – and they had certainly looted plenty of noodles.

The laundry tub in the kitchen struck them as large enough to hold enough for their section and they had it all organised having already sent some scavengers to the Lindenstrasse to hunt down some poultry. It was designed to be a soup which measured up to the joyous defeat of the Germans, it was to be the greatest ever soup. But, with the chaos of the slaughter still reigning in the town, catching a chicken wasn't an easy task.

At the farm where the selected and now well-scrubbed cauldron was waiting to be put to use, one of the Russian lads had come across a hen, in one of the cupboards underneath the staircase, of all places. Here, it seemed, she had valiantly survived the human slaughter while sitting on her eggs. At what turned out to be a fateful moment, she peeked out.

But it was also the moment for another female to make a stand. It was all in the name of protecting one's offspring. The Red Army man, possessed by the vision of his noodle soup, had lunged for the bird completely unaware of the eggs and, proudly clutching in his hand his captured prey, arm stretched high, he crossed the courtyard towards the scullery ready to wring its neck. Little did he expect another female – of the human kind – to block his path: a grandmother!

'Nothing doing! Nix! No killing of cluck-cluck!' she announced, her strong arms on her hips and, wouldn't you know it, the Red Army man instantly dropped the hen, mouth open, as the grandmother – not one to lose the moment - snatched the flapping bird and pressed it to her breast. 'Cluck-cluck now not kaput!' The young Russian was so taken aback that he willingly let himself be taken by the grandmother's hand to be led back like a naughty child towards the cupboard underneath the staircase leading to the cellar. Pushing the cupboard aside, the grandmother

Soviet troops doing what they can to celebrate the approaching end of the war on 9 May 1945, the day Germany's surrender to the USSR was ratified in Berlin and the Soviet Union's official VE-Day.

presented him with the nest of eggs, took one out and held it to the soldier's ears. 'Pip! Pip!' The faces of both grandmother and soldier lit up but the soldier didn't hold back from taking hold of the hen once again, this time, however, to place her gently back down over the eggs before pushing the cupboard into position.

It is worth noting that 'babushkas', no matter which nationality they belonged to, always earned the respect of the Russians. It was no different with this grandmother standing in front of him.

Other chickens in the neighbourhood didn't have such luck, however. Plucked clean and gutted, they were plopped into the cooking vessel, noodles were added towards the end, and a delightful chicken aroma spread through the kitchen.

More and more Red Army men had gathered in front of the scullery from which the fragrant smell of home cooking wafted outside into the spring air. Suddenly we heard an alarm sounding:

all men waiting for the celebratory meal had to line up to report. Swinging themselves onto the open-back lorries, sorrow in their eyes and mouths watering, they were ordered to leave. We could still hear them swearing in Russian.

The column of vehicles had barely taken the turning for Teupitz when the neighbours were already crowding our front door – men, women and children. Rumour has it that they'd never ever tasted a better noodle soup than the noodle soup earmarked to mark the victory of the Soviets.

'Halbe is Worse than Stalingrad!'

Willi Haenecke, ex-mayor of Halbe

Where were my parents? I decided to cross the road and look for them at my sister's. She, along with her husband, had taken over the Haack grocery store in the Kirchstrasse. Everything was upside down when I got to her apartment and nobody was in, of course. I also checked with the neighbours – no success.

Feeling slightly reassured by how quiet it had become in our town, I chose to turn into the Kirchstrasse on my way back. Here the dead, discarded equipment, debris and abandoned vehicles were still strewn around. A gaping hole stared back at me from the church tower. Continuing on, I saw the most frightful scene on what is today the Goetheplatz. Dead soldiers weren't just lying next to each other but on top of each other. Apparently, on seeing this picture of horror and devastation, a Russian sergeant exclaimed that it was worse than anything he'd ever seen before. 'It's even worse than Stalingrad!'

It was much the same at the Lindenstrasse. And I still hadn't come across any milk. Meaning to try my luck at K. Lehmann,

I entered his courtyard. It didn't take me long to realise gratefully that these good people had been spared. Coming towards me was the mother and upon hearing what our situation was at home, she immediately filled my jug with milk. 'Drop by any day,' she said gently, 'I'll always have some milk for you.'

I had been gone for a long while and my family, understandably worried about my whereabouts, were happy to see me return fit and healthy. Realising that I had brought with me some longed-for milk, they were overjoyed.

Around here the war had indeed ended! A little later on we'd hear that on 1 May the Red Army held a rousing victory parade just at the foot of the Teupitz Hills.

The Tasks Ahead

Willi Haenecke, ex-mayor of Halbe

I left the cellar on 2 May 1945. One of the reasons why I left our shelter was to find milk, but also to check the farmstead to see what was still standing. And of course we needed food. If we were to look after the farm we had to be on site and the list of tasks ahead was daunting. Additionally, we wanted to ensure that no intruders would take over our empty home; staying put in that cellar was not an option. We decided, however, not to do anything in haste, not to go straight to the farmstead but rather to be cautious, move slowly and initially just find shelter somewhere close to our house.

Remembering Frau Bredow who used to mind the children for us on the odd occasion that we went out for the evening in the good old times, we got in touch with her. Together with her husband and child she still lived in the upstairs of a house shared with the Bürger family. They took us in despite already being cramped.

As in so many homes, the house was fully occupied not just by the official tenants, but also by refugees. I should also add that the Russian soldiers certainly didn't have an easy time with our women-folk; there was an immediate and loud outcry at every such attempt which immediately drove the lads away. In fact the local Russian commandant strictly prohibited his men from taking such liberties and severe punishment was in store for anyone transgressing the rules.

The commandant asked the town's inhabitants to bury the dead. We dug large pits and laid down the corpses and one such mass grave was located in our garden, between 38 and 39 Lindenstrasse. Strangely, this chore quickly became routine to us – it was as if we'd been doing it all our lives. We didn't do it particularly reverently, nor did we have any reservations or even feel dread, which might have been expected when dealing with so many deceased.

Unbelievable . . . it had taken only a week to create these piles and piles of festering corpses, a week, mind you, the like of which our town's people had never before experienced and which they wouldn't forget for as long as they lived – a week of terror, fear and pain, a week in which families had been torn apart or completely annihilated, and when every day and every night was filled with the din of battle and the air shuddered with the screams of the wounded and the cries of the dying.

On emerging from the cellar, all we could see before us were the dead, only the dead. The survivors were hardly visible; they were quiet, indifferent really, their senses dulled – I'd say they were no longer the same people as before this disaster and it's for that reason that they went about performing the task without displaying any emotion or ill effects, though this was an assignment which normally they would have rejected. The dead obviously needed to be buried for fear of an epidemic breaking out and to get rid of the persistent sickly smell of decay lying over all of Halbe.

It's quite surprising really, what a beaten army leaves behind.

After catching some horses, I harnessed them to carts in which I piled up the dead cattle and horses I found in the stables, before shoving the whole lot into a trench excavated in the village field just before Androw's estate. After that we were ordered to collect the ammunition which was to be blown up near the forestry office, along the road towards Hammer, and we were damn lucky that nothing untoward happened.

One day I decided to take my cart down to the marshy area where I knew that a truly gorgeous stallion was running wild, and sure enough, attracted by my horses, this beauty sidled up to the pair. I simply roped him with a halter which I had taken off a dead horse just before. Carrying on, I drove my cart to a meadow near Löpten and, lo and behold, I came across another cart, this one filled with women's underwear. Ha, I thought, perhaps I should avail myself of some of these goods and take them home; somehow, though, it just didn't sit right with me. Resisting the temptation at first I convinced myself that this wasn't mine to take. But who did it belong to? Finders' keepers? Such were the times . . .

But the day wasn't over yet. At the edge of the forest, I came across several bundles of notes. New, 20-Mark notes as if they were hot off the press. This wasn't the first time I'd seen loads of money just lying around, but I would ordinarily not pick it up, partly because I believed that a change of currency was imminent and any money I owned would instantly be worthless. This time round, I gathered up the notes, wryly thinking that they'd come in handy to wipe my bottom. Frankly, it wasn't hard

. . . there were heaps of them lying around. Eventually, I stopped as I had plenty stacked away; had I continued for another hour, it would certainly have spared my wife worrying later on about our livelihood. Job done, I harnessed my horses and attached the Hindenburg lights [similar to modern tea-lights] to the rear as I didn't want to risk an accident in the dark, seeing as all the road lighting had been shot up.

Once home, I hid the money on a beam underneath the shed roof. Ella, my wife, wasn't home at the time so was quite unaware of this entire event, and later on I totally forgot to tell her about it.

Our day's work usually ended by 4 p.m., at which time we set out into the woods to look for food. While we had plenty of potatoes, we rarely had even a single gram of flour to our name, nor meat nor sausage. Our smokehouse had been plundered, likewise our larder, and the pickled goods stored in the cellar had disappeared. Every evening I'd return from the woods with the back of my bike packed high with anything edible that I had found, above all loaves of bread which mysteriously kept appearing neatly stacked on a lorry, as if intentionally left there for us to find. Tinned food was also free for the taking and more often than not I'd return home with three tins or more. Once I stumbled over twenty typewriters, but left them sitting there apart from one which I hid in the grange . . . to be promptly stolen from there a few days later.

It's quite unbelievable, what a defeated army leaves in its wake. Those not burdened by an incriminating past and sufficiently crafty to pick up any unclaimed goods could easily make a good living for themselves which could last them for a long time. Bartering would come into its own just a few months later. As for myself, I stocked up relatively modestly . . .

A Revolutionary Committee in Action

Willi Haenecke, ex-mayor of Halbe

During the war Social Democrat Party (SDP) and German Communist Party (KPD) members in exile formed a revolutionary committee. One of their goals was to arrest all members of the Nazi Party. It wasn't clear where they were going to be transported to – we guessed it might be Siberia. Opinions about who I was, what my role had been and what my actions were varied widely. At a special committee meeting, seven voted against my arrest and five voted for it, which meant the loss of my position as mayor.

The value of my farmstead didn't mean such a huge amount to me but as I was a farmer through and through I was emotionally attached to it. During the few years managing the farm I had proved my worth and turned a failing enterprise into a thriving estate. However, back in 1943 I had foolishly commented that I would readily give up the farm if that would end this blasted war. Folks obviously hadn't forgotten these words and were determined to hold me to them. Now that the war was over, I was to pay the price. For twelve years, they claimed, I had served as a mayor of Halbe and it was time to move on. Indeed, my family and I were alive and well and, rather than being resentful, I should be pleased and pray that nothing worse might happen, that's what I kept telling myself.

I certainly wasn't the first nor the last person to be forced to start afresh. Ella and I were used to hard work and if that was all it would take, so be it. We would lose the farm, but we would certainly survive the coming years, however tough these might turn out to be. I felt at peace. And yet ... things turned out differently, again.

Every former Nazi Party member in the local area was ordered to report and register at the town hall on 11 May 1945. All party officials had already been arrested – many had never held any significant position with the party but merely carried out minor functions such as collection of membership fees and so on. On that day I had just finished ploughing the field which I had started work on before those fateful days in the cauldron, some half a hectare, and had planted potatoes on the Saturday. The next day, Sunday 13 May, I set out to fence in a small section so that I could feed the cows who'd just calved. The day was very warm and thus I was only wearing my khaki shirt, a pair of trousers and a light jacket. While I was working I was suddenly called away and instructed to report to the town hall, first floor, the mayor's office. I knew the building well of course as it had belonged to my grandmother Klicks.

I had no clue what this was about, but was quite taken aback to see a guard standing at the front of the building. Anxious about what might await me, I climbed the front stairs, and when I became aware of another armed guard sternly watching all the comings and goings, my mind certainly wasn't set at ease. On entering, I took in the familiar surroundings but worried when my eyes fell on the about twenty men already sat waiting there, all previous party members; six more joined us after me. Each one was separately summoned and interrogated in the room opposite. It goes without saying that the atmosphere was pretty gloomy. What would happen to us? We all felt we were doomed. Would we come out of this?

From the window I could still see the field which I had ploughed, and a feeling of a real connection to that property surged up in me. Would this be my last view of it? The outlook over the woods beside the fairground and over the woods bordering my own estate made me feel profoundly sad.

My name was called and I was torn out of my reveries. The Russian interrogator, speaking in German, led me through a room where an officer was sitting at a desk and into the adjoining interrogation room. 'Which functions did the party entrust on you?' Seeing as I had never been given specific functions, I said this question didn't apply to me. Had he asked me for my positions, I would have listed them as one thing was clear to me: that guy knew more about me than I would have predicted. 'Did you belong to some sort of branch?' I first had to figure out what he meant by that and then recalled the SA which was indeed a branch of the party. 'I was leader of the SA.' He looked at me quizzically, which proved that he didn't know everything about me. He stood up and left the room.

On the table lay a document with a list of names followed by a cross. All names except for mine already had the cross inserted, after mine there was a visible gap. It must be true then, I concluded inwardly, that all the others had already been sentenced for arrest. Me being here, I began to hope, was only a formality and all I needed to fear was confiscation, not arrest.

The interpreter came back with the officer and together they studied the list intently, then turned their eyes on me. Though I hadn't understood a thing, by then I sort of guessed what would come next and, indeed, they put a cross next to my name. I'd been sentenced.

Next, he brought me back to where the others were gathered. Two men were sent home: G. because he was still suffering from jaundice and L. because he was needed to install the phone line between Märkisch Buchholz and Halbe for the commandant. The rest of us ended up in the kitchen, crammed together and feeling extremely tense.

I started remembering stuff. I knew this building including, of course, the kitchen from my youth. Those were the days when

I'd be allowed to sit on the garden swing after having brought up wood and coals for Grandma Klicks and she'd tell me stories from her past and offer really helpful advice that would hold me in good stead throughout my life. Was this then the place where my life would end?

That evening, Ella came by to bring me some sandwiches, as I hadn't eaten all day. Nobody knew whether we'd see our families again and towards 2200 hours, heavily guarded, we were loaded onto lorries. Quite a few of us feared that we were headed to the gravel pit, to be lined up and executed . . .

Not all the detainees did return. Willi Haenecke only came home after spending more than two years in a labour camp near Moscow.

Reverence for the Dead?

Eberhard Baumgart

Isn't that the question fellow citizens need to ask themselves when reading the press reports that appeared in the years after the slaughter? Let one of the eyewitnesses who nearly lost his life in the Halbe cauldron offer his response, perhaps an explanation:

'Let us look a bit more closely into the mindset of those who were there. What precisely motivated over one hundred thousand souls locked in the pocket to embark on the break-through battle?

'Was it a matter of "run for your lives"? Was it out of the fear that the Soviets, the winners of the war, would be remorseless in their vengeance? Was it just thoughtless, stupid behaviour? Were people acting under some kind of illusion? Was it all a case of wishful thinking on the part of the Germans?

'Who might be able now to say for sure what precisely caused the individual soldier or refugee to keep on the move and, as if gone berserk, seek ways and means to break out of the pocket at Halbe? What motivated them furiously and desperately to brave one obstacle after another, risk their lives each time? How to explain that some indeed reached safety with the comrades of the Twelfth Army, defying risk and injury and the shortage of ammunition and fuel, regardless of pain and hunger?

'Let us frame the question differently: who actually stood a chance of succeeding?

'To put it bluntly, the answer is those who belonged to regiments, battalions and companies where authority had remained intact and where there was a direct link between order and obedience. That's where the combative spirit triumphed.

'Certainly, many of them were clutching at straws – believing the propaganda, slogans and deceptive assurances which were doing the rounds.

'Then there were the "Seydlitz troops" who we believed had been planted among our men in the ever-narrowing pocket. With a clear-cut mission, they seemed to successfully set about their task of adding to the chaos on the ground by spreading inconsistent and contradictory orders. Then we heard General Busse, the commander of the Ninth Army, addressing his men at a meeting. Prepared to put their lives at risk and continue the battle, these valiant soldiers would fully trust his assurances: "Listen up and hold tight for another two days, soldiers! We'll come through!" That was his message and though portentous we wanted ever so much to believe it.

'Officers meanwhile reported that the American army at the Elbe had halted its offensive and stopped their aerial bombardments of German troops which meant that the Twelfth Army could withdraw from its western front line and push

The Halbe forest cemetery.

through east towards the Ninth Army relatively undisturbed. The men couldn't believe this turn of events and were stunned. The news spread like wildfire.

'And it was indeed the truth: troops and reinforcements from the Twelfth Army travelled in the direction of the Soviet troops encircling Halbe undetected by US airplanes. While the fighters had all but lost faith in the so-called *Wunderwaffen* [wonder weapons], they now put their hopes on a different miracle: the Americans must have come to their senses, they believed, and realised that they had colluded with the devil. Then, rumours of a separate peace having been agreed with the western powers began circulating. Indeed, there was whispering that Germany would enter a pact with them against the Soviets . . .

'There is no doubt that such rays of hope stoked the will of the troops to persevere; it fuelled their desire to cross the Elbe to reach the Americans. This hopeful thinking didn't strike us as mad, neither did the announcements seem hyped up. It didn't seem to us that the Ninth Army was in fact a totally lost cause. Why would we, seeing as there was a historical parallel between the here and now and the events of the Seven Years War that took place in this very same area in the 1760s? Wasn't it the same as when Cossacks rode through Berlin and Potsdam, with Prussia practically already on its knees? Wasn't it the same as when the tsar's wife passed away just in the nick of time? And is it not true that the young tsar recalled his troops and thereby saved Frederick the Great and Prussia from defeat? Hadn't Roosevelt, long-vilified as a German-hater, died just in time? If we stood up as one alongside the Americans, we'd chase Ivan back to where he belonged. We thought we had every good reason to believe that.

'This is precisely what gave rise to the fervent desire to break through the lines of the Red Army up to the Elbe where the Americans were on stand by. The call: "Through! Let's get through! Freedom, Freedom!" echoed the resolve and intent of these men. This was what inspired the German troops to advance irrespective of any losses.

'The resolve displayed by the Ninth Army was also rooted in their first-hand experience of the Red Army's cruelty. It was this certainty and the relentless barbarity shown in the ensuing slaughter which led to the scream "Run for your lives!" reverberating through the ranks, convincing all those who were cowards and lawless plunderers that there was no point in fighting; their only goal was not to fall into the hands of the Soviets. The moment those intent on breaking through met Russian resistance, the moment these demoralised gangs

One of the memorials in the forest cemetery at Halbe.

who had completely given up faced the slightest obstacle, they withdrew and went to ground. Undecided, unnerved and too scared to attack, they were only waiting for reinforcements who had successfully broken through to tag on to, and fervently hoped that those in front of them would take the hit.

'Those who embarked on the break-through ended up having to tackle one battle after another. The minute one obstruction had been surmounted, there was another one ahead of them, and then another. That happened day after day, for sixty long kilometres. The columns came under constant barrages of concentrated fire, shells hailing down, blowing up vehicles, men and armaments. If that wasn't enough, these soldiers were disheartened and insecure as to who might be hiding behind the German uniform of the soldier who just joined their units. Were they friends or foes? Would they share the right information, point you in the right direction?

A ceremony in the Halbe forest cemetery marking the fiftieth anniversary of the end of the war.

'Then there was ignorance of the terrain. It was difficult for troops to find each other or link up with other units without maps. However, what all those lost soldiers wandering around in the forest did know was where west lay. It was the direction from where the battle noises were coming, the thunder of artillery shelling, the detonations and the piercing sound of crushed metal. That's where one would meet up with hardy comrades like oneself, with determined Germans who were minded to succeed in the break-through.

'There were quite a few groups among our troops that consisted of such motivated soldiers, often joined by women and girls who didn't wait to be called upon but volunteered, and who would even take the initiative and arm themselves, fall into rank and file and fight as fearlessly and courageously as their male comrades. Groups of women dressed in uniform would also appear on the battle scene and be heard embarrassing the menfolk: "Get a move on, you cowards! Attack!"

'Even now no one knows how many Ninth Army personnel and refugees in the Halbe pocket managed to breach the encirclement, and we will likely never find out. But it was certainly in the tens of thousands. However, there were also tens of thousands who died a soldier's death and the death toll of the victims who perished due to their indecisiveness or cowardice was also frightfully high.'

A Life-decision for Halbe's Dead

Eberhard Baumgart

Shortly after the dreadful events at Halbe in April–May 1945 a Protestant pastor, Ernst Teichmann, got involved with the town's history, and this would change his life as well.

Teichmann had seen much of the war and its horrors. Visiting Halbe in the summer of 1947 he came across the temporary graves of those who'd perished there, some identified by a simple birch crucifix, others by a rusty steel helmet. Pastor Teichmann was deeply disturbed by the disrespectful way the German dead had been laid to rest. Aghast at the prospect of them remaining nameless, he gathered a few like-minded men and embarked on a difficult and complex journey first to find the graves themselves and then register the burials, though so many were unidentifiable.

For many years the pastor was a thorn in the side of the Communist regime, but he carried on regardless: in quintessential

Lutheran tradition he remained a warrior of God fighting against impiety. Not giving up, he went to great lengths to try to identify the dead, cutting through red tape and fighting the Socialist Unity Party authorities to gain their consent for an appropriate cemetery for these soldiers.

It was quite an uphill struggle as he was up against a firm belief that those shovelled under the sand did not actually deserve any better. And yet:

In September 1951 Pastor Teichmann was allowed to move from Schierke im Harz to Halbe where his responsibilities included the upkeep of cemeteries as well as pastoral care. That year he also started work on having the graves scattered around in Halbe and the surrounding forests transferred to one place so that the dead could be reburied in one central cemetery.

And wouldn't you know it, all of a sudden this war cemetery was just what the Communists needed, and this is the background. In 1952 construction work was carried out on land near the Fürstenwald where previously the Ketschendorf Soviet prison camp was located. When builders were digging the foundations for future apartment blocks, they discovered hundreds of corpses. To avoid any publicity, the area was blocked off to remove the dead as discreetly as possible and the Halbe war cemetery, as yet still not completed, seemed the ideal spot for the regime to bury them . . . but not without putting a twist on it.

Between March and May 1952 more than thirty lorries arrived in Halbe, filled with wooden chests containing the remains of those exhumed in Ketschendorf. The bodies had already decomposed fully and the sight of them was dreadful. The firm tasked with reburying the corpses had no orders to count them carefully, never mind attempt to identify them, and it is, therefore, safe to assume that the numbered ceramic plates placed on the graves are incorrect. But even worse, though not surprising, was the inscription on a plaque, a prime example of how the Communists falsified history: '4,000 victims of the Ketschendorf Concentration Camp perished in April 1945', clearly intended to suggest that here too the Nazis were the perpetrators.

The truth is that between the summer of 1945 and February 1947 some 10,000 people were held in that particular camp of whom approximately half starved to death. A significant number of the inmates were twelve-to-sixteen-year-old lads, who had been arrested under suspicion of having been members of the so-called Werwolf resistance force. It was not until after 1989 that the victims of Ketschendorf were remembered with a memorial indicating that Stalin's Communists had murdered them.

A moment of quiet remembrance in the Halbe war cemetery.

While looking after the war cemetery in Halbe, Pastor Teichmann expressed the wish that on his death he too should be laid to rest there, in the war cemetery. His request was denied. The only place the East German authorities allowed Pastor Teichmann to be buried was in Halbe's civil cemetery which adjoins the war cemetery.

Rumours about Halbe

The war cemetery in Halbe is the largest of its kind in Germany. Some 22,000 soldiers and approximately 2,000 civilians now lie buried there, all killed in those few days of April and May 1945 in the area inside the triangle bordered by Königswusterhausen–Beeskow–Lübben. Among the dead civilians are some of the 6,000 victims of the Soviet camp at Ketschendorf.

Epilogue

Those travelling through the villages and towns of Brandenburg towards the Oder will be struck by the many monuments erected by the Soviets in memory of the battles of spring 1945. Their inscriptions refer to the victims among the Red Army and call on Germans to be grateful for the 'liberation'. These monuments can often be found right in the centre of those towns; the sites are adorned with the Communist red star and enjoy the obligatory careful upkeep set out by German law.

It is important to note that following the break-through battle at Halbe the many thousand German dead had to be buried swiftly for fear of an epidemic. But the German burial teams, under the supervision of Red Army guards, were forced to go far beyond the necessary measures; consciously and with premeditation the memory of the dead would be violated and grave injustice committed not only by shoving them disrespectfully into the soil, but above all by strictly prohibiting Germans from safeguarding the soldiers' service books or identification tags. Those dead 'fascists' should remain nameless! That was the intended aim.

Looking back, and given the same circumstances and conditions, I would join the battle of Halbe a second time if the enemy was the type of Red Army man that I met all those years ago. I was a volunteer when I joined the break-through battle at Halbe and the ensuing slaughter was a nightmare filled with horror and murder which would define the rest of my life.

May the gods be gracious, may they ensure that Russians and Germans never again stand opposite each other in a battle of such magnitude. By letting eyewitnesses get an opportunity to speak in these chapters, I hope I have achieved my aim.

Eberhard Baumgart

Table of Ranks

The table below gives a simplified comparison of rank titles in the Waffen-SS, German Army and the U.S. and British Armies, including all the ranks featuring in the text above. It is not an exhaustive list of all possibilities as many other rank titles existed in all armies, particularly in the NCO grades.

Waffen-SS	Heer	U.S. Army	British Army
Oberstgruppenführer	Generaloberst	General	
Obergruppenführer	General der Infanterie [etc.]	Lieutenant General	
Gruppenführer	Generalleutnant	Major General	
Brigadeführer	Generalmajor	Brigadier General	
Oberführer	No equivalent		
Standartenführer	Oberst	Colonel	
Obersturmbannführer	Oberstleutnant	Lieutenant Colonel	
Sturmbannführer	Major	Major	
Hauptsturmführer	Hauptmann	Captain	
Obersturmführer	Oberleutnant	First Lieutenant	Lieutenant
Untersturmführer	Leutnant	Second Lieutenant	
Sturmscharführer	Stabsfeldwebel	Sergeant-Major	Regimental Sgt.-Maj.
Stabsscharführer	Hauptfeldwebel		Company Sgt.-Maj.
Hauptscharführer	Oberfeldwebel, Oberwachtmeister	Master Sergeant	
Oberscharführer	Feldwebel	Technical Sergeant	Staff Sergeant
Scharführer	Unterfeldwebel	Staff Sergeant	Sergeant
Unterscharführer	Unteroffizier	Sergeant	Corporal
Rottenführer	Obergefreiter	Corporal	Lance-Corporal
Sturmmann	Gefreiter	Lance-Corporal	
Oberschütze, Oberkanonier	Oberschütze	Private 1st Class	Private
Schütze	Grenadier	Private	